# MIND YOUR PAWS

JASON R. TOY

FROM PUPPY TO PERFECT PET

SYNERGY
PUBLISHING GROUP

BELMONT, NORTH CAROLINA

*Mind Your Paws: From Puppy to Perfect Pet*
Jason R. Toy

Published by Synergy Publishing Group, Belmont, NC

Interior formatting by Melisa Graham Creative

Softcover, October 2024, ISBN 978-1-960892-15-7
E-book, October 2024, ISBN 978-1-960892-16-4

# CONTENTS

# INTRODUCTION

Wow! It's exciting to welcome a new dog into your home and life. If you're like most people who choose to get a dog, you have an active lifestyle. Every weekend is packed: different places to go, hikes or runs to conquer, and hanging out with your friends at your favorite social hub. Or maybe you're the family who rushes out the door early in the morning to get to soccer practice or beat the crowds to the hidden waterfall in your favorite national park.

Whichever bucket you fall into, one thing is for certain. You want to include your dog in your family's adventures. But you really don't want the embarrassment of the barking, lunging, and plain bad manners of that neighborhood dog that everyone complains about.

What's the point of getting that new furry family member if you can't take it out in public because it misbehaves as badly as your college friend who always got you kicked out of bars?

Here's the challenge: you just got a new dog, but you don't know how to meet this goal.

Maybe you've tried to train your new dog on your own, by piecing together tips from random blog posts and YouTube videos. Confusing, right?

While surfing the web, you may have noticed that the only thing dog trainers can agree on is that other trainers are wrong. If your approach to learning how to train your dog is "reading blog posts and watching random online videos," good luck because you're going to need it! If you're going to go down that rabbit hole, you may as well try to earn your medical degree from WebMD.

| THIS COURSE | THE INTERNET |
|---|---|
| 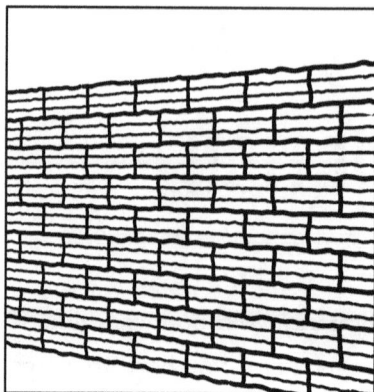 |  |

What you need to turn your dog into the perfect pet is a system that provides consistency and continuity. You'll see much better results, and the furry newcomer to your world will learn more quickly and easily.

This realistic, balanced handbook is for people just like you—people with careers, families, and lives. It contains a step-by-step, proven system that will yield optimum results for both you and your dog, turning your pet into a welcome family member.

Here, you'll find out what actually motivates your dog, rather than what you think motivates it. You'll find a consistent yet flexible approach to training that will result in a contented dog that fits into your lifestyle. Your perfect pooch may even come to rival your favorite child—or your spouse—in your affections.

## Dog Training Today

Let's be honest. We won't be reinventing the wheel on these pages. However, dog training methods have evolved quite a bit over the past five to ten years. My objective is to keep you up to date with current trends and philosophies without sacrificing good ol' quality and reliability. Our goal is to give your dog the freedom it deserves.

I'm a dog lover, dog trainer, entrepreneur, and now an author. And yes, my mom is proud of me! I've owned and operated a dog training school in the Carolinas since 2012. I also get bored quickly, which may be why I relate so well to puppies.

As a dog training professional, I continue to learn the latest approaches and new takes on old training styles that yield different, often better, results. I constantly study the methods others in the field are developing and integrate new methods into my training system whenever appropriate.

Today, dogs are primarily their owners' companions. Although some breeds and lineages are still maintained for their ability to perform certain tasks, this manual focuses exclusively on dogs that are primarily pets—the kind of dog you probably have or plan to get.

## What You'll Learn

This book is broken up into six sections or parts of a few chapters each. The sections deal with the different stages of your dog's journey, helping you understand what you can expect of your dog at each stage.

In Part I, Finding Your Best Friend, you'll learn everything you need to know about choosing a pup. Part II, Puppy Prep, focuses on what you can expect when you invite an adorable bundle of fur and drool into your home. Part III, Welcome Home, sets you up for success from the moment your new family member crosses the threshold.

Part IV, Training Foundations, explains the principles behind training, so you understand *why* your dog does what it does. It's complemented by Part V: The Heads-(P)up, which sets you up to train your dog as kindly and effectively as possible.

Finally, Part VI, Paws to the Pavement—Teaching the ABCs and 123s, is where the rubber meets the road. This is a practical guide to training your dog correctly from the beginning, making your life and theirs easier.

This approach will pace your expectations and reduce possible frustration and regret—especially during those 4 a.m. potty breaks early on. However, you may be picking this book up when your dog is already past certain stages. Don't worry. There's still plenty to learn here. Learning the whole system will make troubleshooting easier. Trying to begin training your dog without addressing foundational behaviors is like baking a cake before it's mixed: messy.

This is a field book to take with you while you're out training your dog. Of course, the process will be challenging at times. But we've got your back. This handbook, along with the carefully curated video course content that goes along with it, will provide you with a complete, systematic training approach for turning your puppy into a perfect pet. You can find the video course at: mindyourpaws.com.

mindyourpaws.com

The road may be rocky at times, but the joy of dog ownership is worth the effort. Training your dog well makes for a happier relationship, fewer problems, and—on a macro scale—it makes the world a slightly better place. Every pup and owner who forms a harmonious connection means one fewer dog at risk of abandonment or antisocial behavior.

Try to score at least (ahem) canine out of ten for your dog training and enjoy the warm glow that comes with satisfying dog ownership.

# PART I:

# FINDING YOUR BEST FRIEND

Size, weight, hair length—oh my! What type of dog is right for you? Consider this the definitive guide to finding the pup that's a perfect fit for your pawsonality. Here, we'll look at different breeds and what you should take into consideration when searching for your new best friend. This is like shopping for a new suit or dress. You need to choose a style that matches your personality, in an appropriate size!

# CHAPTER 1:

# WHAT TO CONSIDER

There are many things to consider when choosing a dog for your family. Above all, remember that having a dog entails a long-term commitment of time, effort, and a great deal of patience!

You're welcoming a new family member into your home. This means—surprise!—you don't come first anymore. Dogs don't just magically behave, potty train, or exercise themselves. That's where you come in. A relationship is one thing you can't outsource.

What's most important is to find the right dog, one that really matches you and your family. If you live on the fifteenth floor of an apartment building, a large dog will go mad trapped in that small space most of the day. By the same token, don't tether a highly energetic dog in a yard all the time, or expect that cute little lapdog to roam happily around a farm. It's much easier to commit to a dog that's compatible with your lifestyle.

A lot of people get rescue dogs from a shelter. Very admirable and noble. But this doesn't solve the bigger issue of homeless or abandoned dogs. The first step in the solution is not putting dogs in a shelter in the first place.

Don't become one of the people who have to surrender a dog because of aggression, allergies, divorce, or because you didn't choose your dog carefully in the first place. Look before you leap. You'll reduce the shelter population simply by taking responsibility for any dog you adopt or purchase.

Okay, now I'm stepping off my soapbox. Do you need to better understand what goes into taking on that responsibility? Here are the basics.

## Time

Any dog is going to demand your time, attention, and patience. You'll need to work at training the perfect pet, and the time commitment is going to be greatest when your dog is young.

To take on a new puppy, you need enough time to give them the attention they need. You also need to be at the right stage of your life. If you've just started a new career or a relationship, do you have the bandwidth to add a pup to your life?

Dogs enhance any occasion. But they need care. If you're used to a life of spontaneous travel, consider whether that's best for your future furry friend. All dogs are pack and social animals. They love attention and don't do well being isolated. Make sure you can give them enough of your time to satisfy that need.

## Space

Do you live in an apartment or a house? If you live in the city, you'll be walking your dog around the neighborhood for exercise, not to mention for #1 and #2. If you have a backyard, it's going to be a lot easier to exercise your dog. Nonetheless, loping around the yard is no substitute for your undivided attention.

Do you belong to a homeowners association? Besides dictating the size of your bushes and the length of your lawn, they often have restrictions on breeds and weights. And, believe me, they won't be bending those rules for you. The same is often true of different municipalities, so check in with city hall.

Remember, this commitment will last longer than most of the relationships you had in your early twenties. When getting a puppy, think about the future. If you're renting a house, you may need to move into an apartment in a couple of years. While it's impossible to factor in all life's challenges, don't let your pet suffer the consequences of poor planning.

## Cost

Be prepared for the costs of owning a dog, even if you adopt. According to the ASPCA, the cost of the first year of dog ownership is over $1,000.[1] Here's a non-exhaustive list of the costs you may incur when you choose to take on a pup:

- Food, food and water bowls, treats, toys, collars, leashes, beds, and crates.
- Grooming, boarding, and travel fees.
- Routine and emergency veterinary care, vaccination, and spaying or neutering.
- Breeder cost or rescue/shelter fees.

## Children

Do you have children? Do you plan to have them? If your child is in an early developmental phase, you may want to wait a while before you get a puppy. Safety first. Kids who are too young to understand how to properly handle pups may grab them and pick them up inappropriately, leading to a lot of behavioral issues down the line (for the dog, not the child). You may want to wait until they're a little older and more mature to get a new pet. It will be easier to set rules and boundaries with both your kid and your dog then. It will also save your sanity.

Reality check: Are you thinking about buying a dog for your kid(s)? Just remember, *you* will be the one going outside to pick up poop. I

---

1. Heather M., "How Much Does It Cost to Have a Dog?" ASPCA Pet Health Insurance, accessed April 19, 2023, https://www.aspcapetinsurance.com/resources/dog-ownership-cost/.

know you told them it's their responsibility, but the buck stops with you. Keep your raincoat handy for when it's wee-wee time during a downpour.

## SUPERVISION

If you have a young child, don't leave them and the dog unsupervised. Make sure your kids respect the dog as much as the dog should respect your kids. Though we don't have a book on training your kids ... dogs' toys are for the dog to play with. Kids' toys are for kids to play with.

## Existing Pets

If you already have a dog or another pet, think about whether they and the new arrival will get along. If the dog you already have is well trained, the trained dog can model behavior for the puppy, especially socialization around playtime and toys. It can help teach your puppy mealtime, potty, and walking routines.

What if your current dog isn't so well behaved? You might find your delinquent pet leads your new pup astray. Before long, both of them are wearing leather jackets and smoking cigarettes behind the bike sheds, and you have two rebels on your hands.

Cats, birds, reptiles—I've seen a lot of dogs get along very well with all types of pets. But that's not to say getting along will be a certainty.

## Allergies

News flash! There is no such thing as a hypoallergenic dog breed, although some individual dogs may cause fewer allergy symptoms than others. Also, dogs don't wear shoes they can take off at the door, which means they track in grass and pollen that can introduce environmental allergies into the home.

What? That's not what you've heard. Your wife is allergic to most dogs but still wants a pet, so you're planning on getting a Labradoodle, Goldendoodle, or some other type of doodle.

A 2011 study published in the *American Journal of Rhinology & Allergy* reveals the amount of dog allergens found in households with dogs does not vary with the breed.[2] In other words, families with "hypoallergenic" dogs are living with the same level of allergens in their homes as people who own non-hypoallergenic canines.

## Your Age

If you're a younger, more active individual, a more energetic dog may fit right in. But for older people or those less mobile, a small, low-energy dog makes a lot more sense. A 2019 article in *Smithsonian* magazine highlighted the fact that more than 4,400 elderly people suffered injuries walking their dogs in 2017 alone.[3]

If you're older, owning a dog can keep you social and mobile, but you don't want that pup to take you on an unscheduled detour to the emergency room. Make sure you choose a dog you can control.

The bottom line is that there are a zillion types of dogs out there. Before you bring one home, think carefully about the kind of canine that's right for you.

---

2. Charlotte E. Nicholas et al., "Dog Allergen Levels in Homes with Hypoallergenic Compared with Nonhypoallergenic Dogs," *American Journal of Rhinology & Allergy* 25, no. 4 (July/August 2011), 252–256, https://doi.org/10.2500/ajra.2011.25.3606.
3. Jason Daley, "Dog Walks Are Good Exercise for Seniors—but Be Careful, Fractures Are on the Rise," *Smithsonian Magazine*, March 12, 2019, https://www.smithsonianmag.com/smart-news/taking-dog-out-leading-more-injuries-older-americans-180971687/.

# CHAPTER 2:

# SO MANY OPTIONS!

Okay, you're ready to take on the challenge of caring for a living, breathing, adorable dog. This is a really big deal.

First, ask yourself why you're getting a dog. Are you looking for a protector? A best friend? A cardio buddy to join you on your daily run? Understanding why you're taking the plunge will translate into finding the best breed and dog for you.

Here's a hint. Looks are far less important than personality. Trends come and go, but dogs are lifetime companions. By the time you read this, another newfangled breed, probably with a name ending with "doodle," will be trending. These fads should be put in the same category as fanny packs, Crocs, and frosted tips.

This book is not about fashion. You, your family, and your dog deserve better, so let's get into some of the more serious and important factors you should consider when choosing your new best friend.

As your grandma said: "It's what's inside that counts."

## Puppy or Adult?

Your first big decision is whether to get a puppy or an adult dog. This may seem straightforward, but each option has various pros and cons. The right answer for you may not be the right answer for your neighbor, or even the right answer for you a few years from now. Let's explore your options.

## Puppies

I consider a dog aged up to a year to be a puppy. Puppies are great because you can start from scratch. It's fantastic to watch a puppy grow with you and for you to be a major part of that molding process.

But puppies are a lot of work. As I'll say over and over again, success follows your efforts. It takes time and energy to train a puppy. There are very few shortcuts.

## Adults

An adult dog usually involves less work. They're often already house trained and, because they're mature, can be a little easier to train. By easier, I mean you'll see results quicker.

Of course, adult dogs may come with some baggage. This includes nervousness, aggression, fears, and phobias. But that's not necessarily something to avoid. Maybe you enjoy a challenge; if so, buckle up, we're here for the road ahead.

## Personality Differences

One great thing about getting an adult dog is that you may already see its personality shining through. As long as you can observe the dog in a non-stressful environment, what you see is typically what you get. Sometimes, when adopting a dog at a shelter or temporary holding area, the dog you're shown will be under a great deal of stress or in poor health. Only after a few weeks of settling will it start showing its true colors.

By contrast, you may be unable to read a twelve-week-old puppy. Nature and nurture are still in the early stages of forming its personality and characteristics. You're rolling the dice.

## Age

There are no age restrictions to consider when adopting an adult dog. You should be aware, however, of where the dog is in its life span.

It may be a little harder to adopt an older dog because after the emotional attachment you'll develop, your time may get cut short. But that's not a reason to pass. You have a chance to make a real impact on the rest of its journey, which will also surely impact yours.

## Size

Dogs come in five general size categories:

- Toy/extra small: up to 12 pounds
- Small: 12 to 25 pounds
- Medium: 25 to 50 pounds
- Large: 50 to 100 pounds
- Extra large: over 100 pounds

A dog's size will correlate to the exercise and activity it requires, as well as with how much it will eat … and poop!

Size and strength also determine how easy a dog will be to control. How comfortable will you be walking a large dog down the street? Small dogs, on the other hand, are more portable. If you're looking for a dog you want to be with you on the road or in the air, you may want to cross large and extra-large dogs off your list.

## Energy Level

Dogs, even within breeds, come with a variety of energy levels:

- **Calm**. These are your typical super-chill hounds. A calm dog's perfect day consists of a good breakfast and a nice long nap, followed by plenty of rest to get their strength back for dinner. Calm dogs tend to suit larger households and older owners.

- **Average**. Medium-energy dogs enjoy socializing and playing games of chase with other dogs. They may occasionally bark or race around the house. However, they'll calm down fairly naturally after five to ten minutes without too much work on your part.
- **High**. A high-energy dog wants to play a lot and will find that ball or toy anywhere you hide it.
- **Crazy**. Working breeds—like police or military dogs—need a job. Typically labeled "high drive," they only have two modes: on and on+.

Breed doesn't necessarily determine energy level. If you're getting a dog from a breeder, let them know what you are looking for. They will know which dogs in a litter are displaying which energy levels. Their job is to help find the right fit for you.

Age will also naturally be a factor in energy level. Dogs are usually most energetic as puppies. As they age, that energy begins to dissipate.

## Grooming Requirements

Dogs that shed need regular brushing, of course. But what most new owners don't realize is that shedding dogs are sometimes easier to care for than their non-shedding counterparts.

A dog that doesn't shed requires frequent trips to the groomer. If you don't keep up with regular brushing and bathing, mats may start to develop. Mats develop when dog fur grows and becomes tangled and wraps around itself, forming tightly wound clumps of the loose dead fur and live fur. If not brushed out, mats continue to trap more fur. Long-haired, shedding dogs are also prone to mats.

Some breeds, such as terriers, can be difficult and require special grooming, known as "stripping," to maintain their characteristic wiry appearance.

Stripping is the process of pulling the dead hair out of the coat of a non-shedding dog, either by using a stripping knife or the fingers. A terrier's hard, wiry coat grows and then sheds as it reaches maximum

length. Hand-stripping coordinates shedding and makes room for a new coat to grow evenly.

## Ear Care

Your pet's ears are a big part of how they communicate and express their individual personality—and they're also adorable! You may want to pet, scratch, and admire those precious, fluffy ears, but don't neglect their care. Ear infections are one of the leading reasons for a trip to the vet.

## Long Ears Need Extra Attention

Dogs with longer ears are more prone to infection because those ears can trap moisture and dirt.

## Pay Attention to Allergies

Just like people, pets can suffer from allergies. Some pets can have worse allergies than others. Pets with allergies are predisposed to ear infections. Excessive scratching precipitated by allergy symptoms can let moisture and bacteria into your pets' ears.

While you're giving your dog his well-deserved ear scratches, check for ear infections every once in a while.

## Mixed Breed

The next major consideration is whether you want a mixed-breed or purebred dog. Let's start with mixed breeds.

### Heinz 57

This endearing term refers to your typical mixed-breed mutt. Mixed-breed dogs don't have a lot of the genetic issues that can come with purebred dogs. They typically live longer and have fewer health issues. Recessive genes don't get carried from parents to puppies, and the resulting animals are more resilient.

Mixed Breed 1          Mixed Breed 2          Mixed Breed 3

### Designer Dogs

Designer dogs are mixed-breed dogs you're paying top dollar for. Catchy names like Chocolate and Vanilla Ice Cream Pups are branding terms meant for emotional appeal. A Labradoodle is a combination Labrador and Poodle, and "Labradoodle" is not a breed registered with the American Kennel Club.

Goldendoodle          Bernedoodle          Labradoodle

## Purebred

The American Kennel Club (AKC) and Canadian Kennel Club (CKC) recognize seven types of purebred dogs. These categories provide a good starting point for understanding the general characteristics of the dog you're thinking of getting, because that type of dog has traditionally been bred for those traits.

The other side of the coin is that not every purebred dog comes out the same way. Have you ever looked at your brother or sister and wondered how on earth they turned out the way they did? Dogs are no different. Any family can accommodate a range of personalities.

However, a dog's breed is a place to start when considering how a dog's personality will end up. Breeds are like paint jobs. Remember colors come in an assortment of hues. You could get any number of different shades of blue.

Buying a purebred is also like buying a car. You may want a Mustang, but there are a lot of models of Mustangs. You could get that very fast racing 5.0-liter engine model. But you could also get a standard four-cylinder Mustang with great gas mileage.

## Sporting Dogs

Sporting dogs have traditionally been bred to flush out and retrieve game birds. They're typically active and alert and work closely with hunters to locate and retrieve game. They love to be in the field and have well-insulated, water-repellent coats. They're very resilient to the elements.

Translation: they've got to get a lot of exercise and enjoy the outdoors.

There are four basic types of sporting dogs: Spaniels, Pointers, Setters, and Retrievers, including Labrador Retrievers.

Labrador Retriever          German Shorthaired Pointer          Cocker Spaniel

## Hound Dogs

Hound dogs ain't nuthin' but a highly diverse category of breeds, which vary enormously. Most hounds share the common ancestral trait of being used for hunting.

Some, called scent hounds, use acute scenting powers to follow a trail. Others, called long winds, demonstrate incredible stamina as they relentlessly run down their quarry. These long-legged dogs are also known as sighthounds or gazehounds, since they hunt by sight.

This category includes Pharaoh Hounds, Norwegian Elkhounds, Afghans, Beagles, and several others. Some hounds, including Beagles, produce a unique howling sound known as baying.

Bloodhound

Dachshund

Greyhound

## Working Dogs

These breeds love their jobs. They're intelligent, quick to learn, strong, watchful, and alert. Some pull sleds or carts, while others guard livestock, homes, businesses, or military installations. They are bred for superior loyalty.

Dogs in this group include Doberman Pinschers, Siberian Huskies, Giant Schnauzers, St. Bernards, and Great Danes. They make great companions, but because they are large and naturally protective, you need to know how to properly train and socialize them. Some breeds

Boxer

Great Dane

Rottweiler

in this group may not be for the first-time dog owner, as they can sometimes be difficult to manage and control.

## Terriers

Terror, I mean terrier, comes from the Latin word terra' meaning "earth." These dogs were originally bred to "go to earth" or dig after small game and vermin, as well as guard their families' homes or barns.

Terriers are feisty, energetic, and eager. Sizes range from fairly small, such as the Norfolk, Cairn, or West Highland White Terrier, to the larger Airedale Terrier. Some popular picks are the Jack Russell Terrier and West Highland Terrier.

Bull Terrier      Scottish Terrier      West Highland White Terrier

## Herding Dogs

Herding dogs were bred to gather, control, and protect livestock. They have an instinctual ability to control the movement of other animals. The herding instinct in these breeds is so strong that they've been known to gently herd their owners, especially the family's children.

Border Collie      German Shepherd Dog      Pembroke Welsh Corgi

In general, these intelligent dogs make excellent companions and respond beautifully to training exercises. They are high-drive dogs that

love to work. They're typically easy to train and are what most general people would consider "smart dogs."

Herding dogs include German Shepherds, Collies, Corgis, and Sheepdogs. Some breeds, such as German Shepherds and Belgian Malinois, are commonly used for police, military and protection work.

## Toy Dogs

A few Toys were bred with a particular purpose in mind, such as hunting rodents. Most, however, were primarily intended to be pampered lapdogs.

Breeds in the Toy group are affectionate, sociable, and adaptable to a wide range of lifestyles. They're smart and full of energy. Many have strong protective instincts. Toy dogs are popular with city dwellers because their small size makes them ideal apartment dogs and terrific lap warmers when nights grow cold.

The Toy category could also be called the cute category, and these dogs are very popular with women (and men) of all ages. Toy breeds include Chihuahuas, King Charles Spaniels, Maltese, Pugs, Toy Poodles, and Yorkshire Terriers or Yorkies.

Chihuahua                    Pug                         Shih Tzu

## Non-Sporting Dogs

Non-Sporting Dogs is a catchall category. This is a diverse group with breeds of varying sizes, coats, personalities, and overall appearance. It's hard to generalize about this group of dogs, which come from a wide variety of backgrounds. Non-Sporting Dogs include three Bulldog breeds, a number of Spitz breeds, three Tibetan breeds, three Poodle varieties, and several more.

There can be vast differences between these breeds, which include the sturdy Chow Chow, the compact French Bulldog, and the foxlike Keeshond. Most are good watchdogs and house dogs. Other breeds in this group are the ever-popular Dalmatian, Poodle, and Lhasa Apso, and the less common Schipperke and Tibetan Spaniel.

Bulldog

Dalmatian

Poodle

Phew! As you've realized by now, there are dozens of different puptions to consider, each one with unique positives and negatives. Now that you've reviewed them, have you decided which one is best for you?

# CHAPTER 3:

# ACQUIRE

Newspaper classified ads used to be the way to find your puppy. Whether you remember those ancient times or not, there are now a lot more options—many based on the breed and age of the dog you want to find.

Some options are better than others. Your contribution to the well-being of pupkind begins when you decide where to get your dog. The goal is to match the right dog with the right owner, or family. When looking for a dog, it's best to focus on your local area rather than looking all over the country! It's important to go meet the dog you're thinking about getting before making any commitment.

Choose to support healthy practices and make the world a slightly happier place for its canine inhabitants, rather than contributing to exploitative practices. Let's sort through your options and figure out where to go and where to avoid.

## Shelters

Not only are you very likely to find a great dog in a shelter, but you'll also feel great about helping a homeless dog find a loving family. Most dogs lose their homes due to owner-related problems like cost, lack of time, allergies, or such lifestyle changes as a new baby, moving, marriage, divorce, or an older owner passing away.

When you pick out a dog at the shelter, you should take it into a neutral territory, so you can explore its personality a bit. Any good shelter will let you do this. A good shelter may actually visit your home with the dog you're interested in.

Most shelters are either run by the ASPCA—the American Society for the Prevention of Cruelty to Animals—the Humane Society, or a county or other local government. The staff working there are trying to do the right thing and find good homes for homeless dogs.

## Rescues

Rescues are usually small groups of volunteers who foster dogs until they find homes. They are networks of caring people who often pull dogs out of shelters where there's a high probability they'll be put down.

### Purebred Rescues

Some rescue centers care for dogs of many different breeds. However, there are numerous breed-specific rescue facilities, dedicated to matching particular types of dogs with loving homes. They take on the responsibility of vetting owners and caring for at-risk animals.

## DON'T GET EMOTIONALLY ATTACHED TOO QUICKLY

Remember that you don't have to fall in love with the first dog you meet. Just like you don't have to buy the first car you look at. It's a good idea to do a little bit of test driving.

## Breeders

Rescues and shelters are great options if you want to give a dog a new lease on life. On the other hand, you may want a purebred puppy. If so, go to a responsible breeder.

How do you distinguish a responsible breeder from an irresponsible puppy mill? We'll cover those in the "Where Not to Buy" section below.

For additional guidance, head to mindyourpaws.com/guides for our checklist to help you identify a reputable dog breeder.

mindyourpaws.com/guides

## Cost

Cost is relative, and choosing a dog is a very individual decision. Older rescue dogs may save money and aggravation compared with puppies, who will exhibit issues like chewing and mouthing all over your beautiful home. But there may be different behavioral issues that require the time and expense of additional training. Getting a dog from a shelter or rescue is different from getting one from a responsible breeder. There are pros and cons with both approaches, and only you and your family can evaluate which one is best for you.

## Where Not to Buy

Knowing where not to buy is just as important as knowing where to buy. Puppy mills, puppy brokers, and even pet stores exploit dogs.

We need to stop supporting these outlets and their practices by withholding our purchasing power to put them out of business. Here are the facts.

### Puppy Mills

Puppy mills treat dogs like livestock. They put profit over the health and well-being of the dogs they breed and sell.

Don't get confused. Puppy mills can be large or small. Just because it's a small household operation doesn't mean it's not a puppy mill. They're often concentrated in rural areas. Sometimes they're even licensed by the Department of Agriculture.

Puppy mills keep breeding parents in cages throughout their lives. Mothers who are no longer able to reproduce are put down. The dogs get no veterinary care, and puppies are generally taken from their mothers too early, which creates serious health and behavioral issues.

These people are evil.

Unfortunately, you typically don't know which breeders are puppy mills. Puppy mills often sell dogs to puppy brokers, pet stores, and on the internet, so be sure to visit any puppy you're considering at its local breeder before purchasing.

## YOU CAN MAKE A DIFFERENCE

You can—and should—stop supporting these practices. Removing demand is the only way to put these people out of business. If you want a good dog, be a good owner. This is your first step.

To learn more about puppy mills and brokers, visit mindyourpaws.com/book/resources.

mindyourpaws.com/
book/resources

### Puppy Brokers

Like puppy mills, puppy brokers' businesses are based on volume. Brokers focus on selling hundreds and hundreds of dogs at a time. Think of them as pyramid network-marketing schemes or used-car dealerships.

Yes, it's possible to get a good dog from a puppy broker. But, more likely, you'll get a puppy with serious health, temperament, or genetic issues, because of the way it's been raised and taken from its mother too early.

With a little research, puppy brokers are pretty easy to spot. They usually sell multiple styles of the current fad dog online. Brokers won't let you meet the puppy's parents or breeder. They promise health and pedigree guarantees, then give you incomplete or missing paperwork.

Puppy brokers often set up shell buildings that you can visit to meet the puppy you're thinking of buying. They choreograph the initial meeting in a well-decorated space where they can show you a cute little puppy.

Like with a used-car dealership, once you walk out of a puppy broker's, the sale is final. If you end up with a goof like Beethoven, Marley from the movie *Marley and Me*, or Santa's Little Helper from *The Simpsons*, you'll be on your own with a delinquent dog. And believe me, behavioral issues are much more amusing in the movies.

## Pet Stores

It used to be common for people to buy their dogs at pet stores. But it's been a long time since the song "How Much Is That Doggie in the Window?" was a hit in the early '50s, and things have changed.

Some pet stores still sell pets as well as food and supplies. Beware, however, since pet stores usually get their dogs from puppy mills or brokers. The goal is to sell as many dogs as profitably as possible, rather than to care for them and make sure they're placed in the right homes.

The US Department of Agriculture (USDA) has several requirements for any individual or organization that sells dogs to pet stores, such as a standard of care when transporting the animals. But puppy mills and breeders consistently break those rules.

Although it's less common to buy dogs at pet stores nowadays, you should also look at the internet as a pet store. Websites that sell dogs and other pets are the updated version of the brick-and-mortar pet store. Think of them as Pet Store 2.0.

You really have to do some research on websites that claim to be run by a breeder or a network of breeders. One of the best ways to do this is to contact the ASPCA or the Humane Society.

## Do Right by Your Dog

It's easy to be seduced by the cuteness of puppies and forget to think about where they come from, how they've been treated, and what type of practices you're supporting by purchasing them. Don't make that mistake. You may only be welcoming one dog into your family, but by choosing to support shelters, rescues, or responsible breeders, you send a clear message about how you believe our canine friends deserve to be treated.

If you're thinking about a certain breed or style of dog, talk to friends or family members who have one. Or go to a dog meet-up group, either in person or by seeking out breed-specific groups online. This will give you the chance to talk with other owners and get their insights. Doing a little homework will really pay off in giving you a clue about what you're getting yourself into.

# PART II:

# PUPPY PREP

This part of the book provides you with all the goss on what to expect when you are expeting. Like any other new arrival, dogs go through predictable life stages, from adorable newborn to rebellious teenager. In this part of the book we'll explain the growing pains you can expect as a new pawrent, with a particular focus on the crucial first twelve weeks. Naturally, you'll want to know how to handle the initial honeymoon period, when all you want to do is gaze you're your angel's eyes and tell them how gorgeous they are, and—perhaps even more importantly—puppy proofing, so you can prolong the feels when the initial glow wears off. Finally, we'll give you a comprehensive list of what to have on hand throughout the adventure.

# CHAPTER 4:

# PUPPY STAGES

Puppies are adorable, which is lucky for them, because they're also destructive! Whether it's jumping on the counter or chewing the furniture—name it and your puppy will give it a try.

Here are some general guidelines on what you can expect to encounter as your puppy grows, so you know what you're getting into.

## 0–2 Weeks

The first two weeks of a puppy's life are called the neonatal or newborn stage. At this age, puppies can't hear or see, although they do have the senses of touch and taste. They don't have any teeth and can't regulate their own body temperature.

Neonatal puppies sleep almost all the time. Their mother takes care of keeping them warm and feeding and cleaning, just like a mother would with a newborn baby.

## 2–4 Weeks

This is a transitional stage, during which puppies start opening their eyes and responding to light and movement as well as sound. They also develop the all-important canine sense of smell.

Although they're still on mother's milk, they start developing their first set of "baby" teeth. They'll begin recognizing their mother and littermates.

At this point, puppies start to become mobile. They're able to stand but will also stumble a lot, crawling instead of walking. They also start wagging their tails and barking a little.

## 4–12 Weeks

From four to twelve weeks, the puppy starts building relationships and forming social boundaries and hierarchies—dominant and submissive. From this point, the way it interacts with people and other puppies has a strong influence on the dog it will ultimately become.

The puppy's littermates become more important from four to six weeks, and so does play. It learns bite inhibition or soft mouth—the ability to explore with its mouth without causing injury. During this time, a puppy will develop a lot of curiosity and begin seeking out new experiences. By five to seven weeks, it needs lots of positive human interaction.

This is why it's crucial to select a good breeder. Puppy mills are like canine factory farms, churning out pups and raking in the profits, with little concern for the well-being of the dogs. A good breeder cares for their little bundles of floof, and typically lives in an environment where the pups get a chance to socialize with family and potential buyers. This is much healthier for the dogs, and also means you're more likely to get a happy, well-adjusted pupper than an emo hound.

### Early House Training

By seven to nine weeks, a puppy has full use of its senses and is refining its coordination. It can begin to be house trained at this point. Breeders start this with paper training, laying down paper where the dog goes to the bathroom.

This approach helps ensure the puppy's safety. The soil outdoors contains a lot of bacteria, so most breeders put paper down in little plastic pools or on concrete. They can then disinfect these areas to keep puppies as healthy as possible.

## Fear Stage

Stranger danger! There's often, though not always, a fear stage from eight to eleven weeks. Puppies start becoming afraid of everyday objects and experiences, often things they were totally fine with up to this point. The puppy's fear is usually random. Support and positive reinforcement are what will get it through this phase.

Use lots of food rewards as leverage. If your dog gets anxious in a certain spot, you can feed it meals there to help work through that fear.

## WHEN TO GET YOUR PUPPY

Most people get a puppy at eight to twelve weeks. Twelve weeks is preferable, since this gives the dog more time to socialize with its mother and littermates. Since most dogs go home to single-dog households, waiting a bit gives the puppy a little more time to learn from its pack of siblings.

Many people believe they shouldn't socialize their new furry companion until the dog has had all their shots. In fact, the American Veterinary Society of Animal Behavior (AVSAB) states that, "In general, puppies can start puppy socialization classes as early as seven to eight weeks of age. Puppies should receive a minimum of one set vaccines at least seven days prior to the first class and a first deworming. They should be kept up-to-date on vaccines throughout the class."[4]

---

4. American Veterinary Society of Animal Behavior, "AVSAB Position Statement on Puppy Socialization," 2008, https://avsab.org/wp-content/uploads/2019/01/Puppy-Socialization-Position-Statement-FINAL.pdf.

# 3–6 Months

This is often called the ranking period because dominance and submission within the household "pack," including you and your family, is fully established at this stage. You can also think of this time as your puppy's elementary school phase.

Like human children, dogs at this point are very influenced by their human and canine playmates. Your puppy's playgroup may also now include other species, like cats and birds.

Take advantage of your puppy's dependence and strong desire to be near you. You can really leverage this when you start serious training. However, you can also expect your puppy to test the limits of your patience at this time. Only one of you will come out on top.

## Full House Training

Around twelve weeks of age, puppies begin to be able to better control their bladders and bowels. They may start sleeping through the night without potty breaks or accidents.

https://potty.app

House training should start to go more smoothly now. Most dogs can be fully house trained at the age of four to five months. Remember that it's important to keep a regular house-training schedule. Consistency is key. If all this sounds overwhelming, check out the website https://potty.app for the quick 'n' dirty guide to nailing potty training.

## Teething

Puppies get their "baby teeth" at about three to four weeks. From three to six months, the baby teeth fall out, and adult teeth start coming in. When this happens, expect your puppy to start teething and chewing.

It's especially important to puppy proof your house at this stage. Hide or place anything you don't want to get chewed out of reach, as well as anything that might cause choking or other hazards, such as power cords or toxic plants.

Give your puppy lots of chew toys, so it won't need to satisfy its urge to chew on the living room rug or your favorite shoes.

## SINGLE-EVENT LEARNING

During a dog's fear period, there's no need to use force to get through an issue. This can intensify the dog's fear reaction, often permanently.

Ultimately, the fear period is a survival mechanism. In the wild, a young wolf must quickly learn to stay clear of predators without needing multiple near-death experiences to absorb the lesson or its first encounter may be its last.

## 6-12 Months

A puppy's adolescence usually starts at six months. You can expect many of the normal teenage problems during this phase. Brace yourself!

Your puppy's growth will begin to slow down. However, it will also have increased energy and become more willful.

Things can start getting a little "hairy" at this point, even with the best preparation. As your puppy becomes an adult, it has a very high need for stimulation, companionship, and nearly constant activity. Its tolerance for boredom and inactivity is very low.

Your growing puppy will become increasingly confident and independent at this time. Motivated by its increasing curiosity, it will start venturing farther and farther from your side.

## Chewing

Many dogs go through a second chewing stage between seven and twelve months. As they now have their adult teeth, this isn't a teething issue. These displays of destructive behavior are often caused by increased energy and confidence, as well as the flip side of these—boredom. Chewing becomes the dog's default way of making life more interesting.

We'll be dealing with what to do during this period in later chapters on training. As a preview of coming attractions, it's a great idea to use a crate until your dog is a year and a half old to avoid problems during both the teething and chewing phases.

## Second Fear Stage

Another fear stage can start between six and fourteen months. Not all dogs experience this, but some do. This should be dealt with much as you dealt with earlier fear phases: through reassurance and attention.

## Sexual Maturity

Dogs become sexually mature between six to twelve months. They get to skip the acne and facial hair, but they do experience significant hormonal changes that can alter their behavior.

Your dog will probably become more willful at this stage. It can also become a little crankier or super rambunctious. It may exhibit just plain weird behavior and seem to have forgotten its training.

Hormone levels directly influence this. It's like having a teenager in your house. And, like with a teenager, you have to remain firm and consistent. The difference is that your adolescent dog will eventually mind what you say!

# 12–18 Months

Between twelve and eighteen months, your puppy will reach physical and emotional maturity. By the time it reaches its full size, your dog is physically mature. Like unruly teenagers, however, dogs mature sexually before they reach physical maturity. Sexual maturity starts around six months of age, while physical maturity takes a year for smaller breeds and up to two years for larger ones.

Unlike humans, this phase isn't evidenced by a desire to read *The New York Times*, or an abundance of decorative pillows, but you'll see clear signs.

Once its adult personality begins to emerge, your dog will stop pushing boundaries in hopes of raising its status in the pack. Instead, it will listen and respond better to social cues from you and other dogs.

Now that you know more about what to expect during your puppy's various phases, it's time to start getting ready to welcome your new family member into your home. Puppy proofing, as it's called, should be done before you get your dog—not after.

# CHAPTER 5:

# FINDING AND GOING TO THE VET

Over the course of your puppy's first six months, you'll see a lot of your vet. You want to build a relationship that will continue into your dog's adulthood.

## Referrals, Reviews, and Interviews

Referrals are the best way to go about finding a vet. Talk to your pet-owning friends and family and ask if they have had good experiences with their vets. Online reviews can also be helpful. But take these with a grain of salt. Don't eliminate a possibility just because of one or two bad or disgruntled postings.

Don't hesitate to call and visit vets you're thinking about. Usually, it's best not to bring your dog along on the first visit. Bringing your dog to several different clinics will probably just make them nervous.

Most people judge vets by their bedside manner, which is really important. Although bedside manner may not directly correlate with quality of care, you should feel comfortable asking questions. Over time, it's essential to be able to build a good, trusting relationship with your vet.

These initial interview visits can serve several purposes. Vets are great resources. You may have questions about a breeder or about

mindyourpaws.com/guides

45

local pet restrictions and laws, which the vet you're interviewing should be able to answer.

## Convenience and Emergencies

Two other important things to look for are convenience and emergency hours.

Convenience involves both location and scheduling. Those last-minute vet trips should involve a minimum of driving.

There are special emergency veterinary hospitals. But some vets' offices also serve as hospitals and emergency clinics. It's nice having a one-stop shop where your dog can have regular visits and also be taken in case of emergency.

But this isn't always possible. A general practitioner may need to refer you out to specialists to tackle complicated issues. If your vet's clinic doesn't have emergency hours or an in-house specialist staff, make sure they have a solid and extensive referral network.

## Vaccinations and Medication

The first thing you should go to your vet for after getting a puppy is vaccinations. Vaccinations are as important for dogs as they are for humans. Ignore anyone who tells you otherwise—including your dog's breeder.

Dogs love to lick puddles and often put disgusting things in their mouths. Puppies especially do a lot of exploring with their mouths, and it's easy for them to pick up diseases.

To know when to vaccinate, speak with your vet.

And if there is heartworm in your area, be sure to have your vet treat your dog with the proper medication. Mosquito bites can spread the parasite that causes heartworm.

Often, you can get heartworm medication in combination with flea and tick medication. Tick medication stops ticks from latching

## VACCINATION SCHEDULE

Speak with your veterinarian about the best ways to protect your pup.
Factors like lifestyle and state regulations may impact your treatment.

### 8-10 WEEKS
- Distemper
- Hepatitis
- Parvovirus
- Parainfluenza

Can be combined

### 12-14 WEEKS
- Bordetella
- Distemper
- Hepatitis
- Parvovirus
- Parainfluenza

Can be combined

### 16-18 WEEKS
- Bordetella
- Distemper
- Hepatitis
- Parainfluenza
- Parvovirus
- Rabies

Can be combined

### EVERY 1-3 YEARS
- Distemper
- Hepatitis
- Parainfluenza
- Parvovirus
- Rabies

Can be combined

A booster is recommended for dogs 6 months - 1 year without a vaccine history

onto your dog's skin and stops the diseases, like Lyme disease, that ticks transmit.

## Don't Forget Dental Care

Dental care is something most dog owners mistakenly forget about. But there's a direct correlation between healthy teeth and your dog's life span, since a lot of diseases come through the mouth. A mouth that hasn't been cared for, with bad teeth, leads directly into the rest of the body. Though often overlooked, dental care is very important to your dog's health.

## Spay & Neuter

Unless you're a professional breeder—which you aren't—your dog should be spayed or neutered. Right? Absolutely!

At the same time, it's important to note that fixing your dog isn't the panacea everyone once thought it was (i.e., for aggression or excitement issues). Want to prevent aggressive behavior? There's no substitute for proper training and exposure at the appropriate life stages.

Choosing a vet with whom you feel comfortable and getting to know them is essential for you *and* your new puppy. In a best-case scenario, you could be opening a relationship that will last for more than a decade. Invest some time up front and save yourself a lot of headaches further down the road.

# CHAPTER 6:

# PUPPY PROOFING

Your puppy is adorable. But it can also jump, climb, chew, and scratch. Meaning you'll need to puppy proof your home, removing destructible items from harm's way.

Puppy proofing also involves stocking up on supplies you and your new dog will need—everything you need to do to make your home ready for the new family member.

## Essential Supplies

This essential supplies checklist includes many items that will last your puppy into adulthood. However, others will need to be replaced as your puppy grows.

For more information on how to order these supplies, visit mindyourpaws.com/shop.

mindyourpaws.com/shop

### Kennel/Crate

A kennel/crate is going to make both your puppy's and your lives easier and safer.

#### Size

When buying a kennel or a crate, height and length are the most important measurements to consider.

- Height: Measure your dog from the feet to the top of the head. Then add two to four inches to determine how high its crate needs to be.

- Length: Measure your dog from the nose to the end of the tail. Then add two to four inches to this dimension to determine recommended length.

Choosing the size of a crate is a balancing act. You can purchase a kennel or crate in a larger size for the future—one that will fit your dog when it's fully grown. Then, you can block it off to make it puppy-sized.

You don't want to leave too much space in the crate, otherwise your puppy can go to the bathroom, then lie down and sleep in another corner. On the other hand, you want the crate to be large enough for your dog to stand up, turn around, and lie down comfortably. When in doubt, go for the slightly larger option.

### Styles

Different styles of crates include wire, plastic, soft-sided, heavy-duty, and designer. Each type suits different dogs and family circumstances, so there's no single right answer to the question: "What type of crate should I buy?" In this section, we'll dive into the different types and explore the positives and negatives of each.

*Wire crates:*
- Pros: Great ventilation. Wire crates usually come with a divider, so you can section the crate off as your puppy starts to grow. Most of them fold flat for easy storage or travel. They have a removable floor tray that's great for cleanup—and you better believe you'll need to clean up.
- Cons: Because they're foldable, they're easy to break out of, so are not great for mini canine Houdinis. Also, they're wide open, so if you put a crate in a busy room, your dog will be able to see everything that's going on.

*Plastic crates:*
- Pros: For dogs who like cozy places, or who sleep in corners or under tables. They're great for airline travel. They're also more

difficult for escape artists to MacGyver their way out of. Plus, they come in different designer colors!

- Cons: Not well ventilated and hard for dogs to see out of. They're also harder to clean. If there's a major incident, you may need to get out the garden hose.

*Soft-sided crates*

- Pros: Very lightweight and portable, making them great for travel and easy to store.
- Cons: Difficult to clean up potty accidents. Also, if you have a destructive dog or a chewer, the crate has no chance. It'll be "dog one, crate zero."

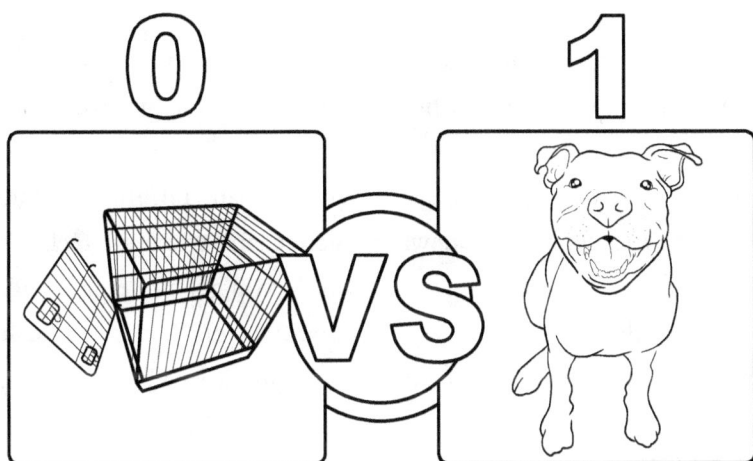

*Heavy-duty or professional crates*

- Pros: Great for destructive dogs or escape artists. Some are approved for airline travel.
- Cons: Often very expensive. However, factoring in the cost of a dog getting out and possibly damaging your home, the cost evens out.

*Designer crates*

- Pros: Fit in with your décor, and can even be used as side tables or other pieces of furniture.

- Cons: Wood floors easily damaged by potty accidents and not good for big or destructive dogs. Also, generally expensive.

## Baby Gate

Baby gates are generally used to baby-proof a house and are frequently put at the top or bottom of staircases. They're also used to close off sections of the house to confine a baby to a certain room or area.

That's how baby gates are used with puppies—for confinement, and for keeping puppies safe from stairs and separated from other pets.

## Bowls

You'll need high-quality water and food bowls for your dog to eat and drink out of. Get a set for home and possibly a lighter weight set for travel.

Choose something that will last. There are many different options, including plastic, ceramic, stoneware, silicone, and stainless steel.

Don't skimp on food and water bowls. If you get something cheap, chemicals can leech into your dog's food and water. Your dog's health depends on what it eats out of, so get high-quality bowls.

## Exercise Pen

Exercise pens are generally open at the top and bigger than crates. They're usually made of metal wire or plastic. They're easy to move around and to fold for storage.

Exercise pens are great tools. They contain your dog, but, unlike a crate, give it plenty of space to move around and play. You can think of them as playpens for your dog. They're great babysitters and mean you don't have to crate or tether your puppy constantly to keep it out of trouble.

Working in your home office and want your dog to hang out with you, but you can't give it your full attention and don't want it chewing up your cables or papers? Or you have kids, and it's time to make dinner? You can set up the exercise pen in the office or kitchen and have the puppy around without it getting underfoot and in the way.

## Food

It's a no-brainer: giving your dog high-quality, nutritious food is important for its health and well-being.

There are many different dog-food types, including dry, wet, canned, frozen, and raw. There are also special diet options. There are pros and cons to each choice, and obviously you can mix and match. Convenience will play a big role in your puppy's care and feeding.

## FINDING THE BEST FOOD FOR YOUR PUP

How do you find the best quality canine chow? Unfortunately, there hasn't been a lot of good scientific research done on dog food. A lot of opinions about dog food, as with human food, are based on whoever is paying for the study.

You have to do your own research and come to your own conclusions. But how?

The most reliable dog-food resource I have found is Dog Food Advisor, which breaks down dog food into many different categories. The site provides independent ratings based on the content of the food and provides editor's choices, highlighting the best in class. Dog Food Advisor also lists recalls, so you know if an issue arises with your chosen brand.

mindyourpaws.com/
book/resources

## Leashes

A leash is a simple and effective way to control your dog. It goes without saying—or should—that a leash is the best tool for taking your dog safely out of your house and away from your property. Here are the options.

### Standard Leash

Everyone is familiar with the standard flat leash with a clasp at the end. It's the most common leash used for everyday walking and basic training. They're made from a wide variety of materials, like cotton, nylon, and leather.

They're generally four to eight feet long, and clip onto your dog's collar. Standard leashes made of round, rope-like material are another popular choice, and there are also leather and vinyl versions.

A good quality standard leash works well with all dogs, because they come in various thicknesses and strengths. When properly fitted to your dog's size, they provide maximum safety and control. The six-foot standard leash is particularly recommended, as it isn't too short but gives more control than the eight-foot version.

## METAL LEASHES

Metal leashes are a variation on and great replacement for standard leashes. They're very useful if you have a dog that likes to chew or destroy its regular leash.

Metal leashes are made of interconnected metal links. A metal leash is a great tool that helps to alleviate destroying standard leashes.

There are a couple different options for clasps. Look for nice, secure metal ones. If you get a leash made of fabric, make sure the stitching is high quality.

### Slip or British Lead

A slip leash or British lead is a rope-style leash that has a built-in collar. You slip on the collar and then grab hold of the leash end.

Slip leads are great for controlling escape-artist dogs. For the safety of the dog, most vets and groomers exclusively use slip leads. Slip leads are a super-convenient way to leash your dog quickly and easily. They're also great for dogs that try to pull out of their leash, since, when the dog pulls, they tighten, preventing those escape artists from wriggling free.

## BUNGEE AND STRETCHABLE RUBBER LEASHES

Bungee and stretchable rubber leashes may seem like a good idea. Their manufacturers tell us they gently correct pulling issues by reducing stress on the leash.

Proper feedback, however, comes not from the leash but from the owner on the other end. A stretchable leash's constant tension desensitizes your dog to leash pressure and negates your ability to train and manage your dog.

In leash training, the primary reinforcer should be no tension at all. When the dog pulls, it should feel tension that it learns to release by returning to your side.

## Long Lines or Check Cords

A long line, or a check cord as it's sometimes called, is a leash that's twenty-five feet or longer. They're great when you're training in your backyard or outdoors.

Long leashes give dogs distance and freedom. But they still allow you to keep your dog tethered in case of an emergency or when you need to work on recall—that is, getting the dog back to you.

Check cords don't retract. If you want to vary or shorten them, you need to use your hands.

## RETRACTABLE LEASHES

Retractable leashes are very popular. But so were parachute pants. A dog on a retractable leash can wander as far as twenty-five or thirty feet from the small plastic handle you hold. A mechanism in the handle allows you to lock, release, and retract the leash. But this offers only the illusion of control, as the mechanism doesn't assure a quick, precise response to dangerous situations.

These leashes offer dogs a deceptive freedom—enough freedom to get in trouble. Effective training requires being clear about your expectations, and retractable leashes don't set definite boundaries. It's very hard to fix a problem that occurs when your dog is thirty feet away from you.

While retractable leashes are ineffective and dangerous, there is a limited place for them. If you live in an apartment and have a young puppy you're taking out to go to the bathroom, you might want to give it some freedom. But in general, retractable leashes aren't good training tools for walking or general obedience.

## House Line

A house line is a leash with the more typical length of four to six feet. However, it doesn't have a loop on the end you hold in your hand. This means your dog can wear the leash at all times, even when you're not controlling it, since you don't have to be afraid of a trailing loop getting caught on your furniture.

House lines are great tools for controlling your dog during training times, as well as keeping an eye on your dog in the house. It's recommended your dog wear a house line until it's potty trained and has passed through its chewing phase.

This type of leash prevents you from getting involved in an unwanted game of chase when your pup grabs something it's not supposed to have in its mouth.

## Collars and Harnesses

The many different collar and harness options include:

- **Traditional flat collar**, which can have either a snap or buckle attachment. This is the option you'll probably start out with.
- **Martingale collar** consists of two loops, one larger and one smaller. Your dog's head goes in the larger loop and the leash attaches to the smaller one. If your dog pulls, the collar will tighten enough to prevent it from slipping out without choking.
- **Head halter** also has two loops. One goes around your dog's muzzle and another around the dog's neck. The leash attaches to the muzzle, redirecting your dog and preventing it from pulling ahead of you.
- **Back-clip harness** fits around your dog's chest and clips on its back. These are great for small dogs, since they don't restrict their throats and airway, preventing more delicate pets from possible trachea damage.
- **Front-clip harness** has a very similar design to the back-clip harness, except that it clips to the chest. It helps prevent minor pulling if your dog needs help walking with a loose leash.

- **Slip or choke chain** should only be used under the supervision of a reputable dog trainer.
- **Pinch or prong collar** should, again, only be used under the supervision of a qualified trainer. These collars are made up of metal links, and each link has a set of metal prongs extending out from it.

## COLLARS AND UNSUPERVISED DOGS

Always remove any collars when you aren't supervising your dog, for example, when it's in its crate, or when you are not home. Special breakaway collars have a safety buckle that releases in emergencies, reducing your dog's chance of injury.

## Grooming Tools

Grooming your dog doesn't only help your dog look better—as important as that may be when you're walking it around the neighborhood. It also reduces your pet's chances of skin and other health problems. Cleanliness equals health!

Grooming helps avoid matting, which can cause skin irritation and trap bacteria in the coat. It also helps avoid thrush, which is a fungal infection that can get in a dog's mouth, nose, ears, and genitals.

When you groom your dog, check for cuts, swelling, lameness, or changes in temperament, all of which could mean your dog is ill.

We've already talked about how important it is to be able to bathe and groom your dog yourself, even if you use a dog groomer. It's also critical for you to work through any of your pet's grooming fear and phobia issues before sending it to a professional groomer.

### Brush and Comb

There are several different styles of brushes and combs:
- **Bristle brushes**, which are great for shorthair breeds.

- **Pin-style brushes** with rounded tips, which are also good for shorthairs.
- **Boar or synthetic bristle-style brushes**, which work well for dogs with dense hair.

### Nail Clippers and Sanders

Typically, if your dog is taking normal walks and running around outside, its nails will grind themselves down. Unlike cats' nails, dogs' nails don't usually get too long and sharp.

However, you may want to trim and shorten your dog's nails, which is where nail clippers and sanders come in. These days, most professional dog groomers use rotary sanders, but clippers can also do a great job.

### Soap and Shampoo

Use high-quality—meaning gentle and non-toxic—soap and shampoo. Some dogs have skin allergies. Also, your dog may lick its fur while you're washing it and ingest some of whatever soap or shampoo you're using.

### Deodorizer and Neutralizer

Hey! Accidents will happen! Which is why it's important to have a neutralizer or deodorizer to help prevent the dog from going to do its business in the same spot over and over and over again.

As long your pet can smell its scent, it will continue to return to the "oops" zone, which is just what you want to prevent. A good odor neutralizer doesn't just remove a bad smell—although that's an important part of its job.

If you need more advice on the best way to remove pet stains and odors, visit mindyourpaws.com/book/resources.

mindyourpaws.com/book/resources

## Poop Bags and Scoopers

One of the essential, not-fun chores of owning a dog is its daily output. Be a good neighbor and pick up after your dog, and don't forget to clear your yard before someone, like you, your kids, or your guests, steps in something they'd rather not have stuck to their shoe.

The poop bag is both the humblest and perhaps most important of all doggie supplies. For minimum unpleasantness and maximum effectiveness, get a pooper scooper as well.

### BACTERIA AWARE

Did you know that a single gram—that's 1/28th of an ounce—of dog poop contains 23 million so-called fecal coliform bacteria? It might be easy to joke around about this, but it's not really a joking matter. Some of these bacteria are known to cause intestinal illness, including cramps and diarrhea, as well as kidney disease in humans.

Dog poop can also contain ringworms, roundworms, hookworms, and whipworms. Ugh. Clean up after your mutt. The health you save may be your own!

## Dog Bed

Dog beds, like most pet supplies, come in a dizzying variety of types and styles. Your dog's sleeping style and where it likes to rest will be the main factors in selecting a comfortable bed.

### Pillow or Cushion

The pillow or cushion style is the basic or standard dog bed. It comes in a huge variety of colors, styles, and designs, with lots of different fill options.

## THE FIRST BED

Don't go crazy selecting your puppy or dog's first bed. Like your teenager's first car, there will probably be a learning curve and some repairs involved. New puppy owners spend lots of money on a very cute dog bed when their puppy is twelve weeks old. That $150 bed gets torn to shreds quicker than a marriage contract in Vegas.

### Elevated Cot

If your dog likes to rest outdoors, you may want to consider a cot-style bed. These are elevated to keep your dog off the hot ground in summer and the cold ground in winter.

Many dog cots are made of a waterproof fabric, which simplifies cleaning. Their sturdy frames make them ideal for larger dog breeds and chewers.

Cots are good for teaching dogs the basic "place" or "spot" command we'll cover later.

### Donut or Bolster

Does your dog like to curl up or cuddle with its head resting on something elevated? Then the donut or bolster bed is for you.

These beds can be round, oval, rectangular, or square-shaped. They feature cushioned bottoms and raised sides that make them look a little like donuts. The "hole" is the ground-floor bed where the dog's torso rests.

### Orthopedic

Orthopedic, mattress-style beds provide tons of support for older pets, or pets with back, hip, or joint issues. They help your pooch avoid pressure points and sore spots.

Older dogs often get hot spots on their hips or other bones when lying on the ground or other hard surface. Orthopedic beds are nice and thick enough to provide cushioning to prevent this.

### Cave

Cave beds are great for dogs that like to nest or burrow under blankets. A popular brand called Snoozer, which was the first to come out with the style, made cave beds very popular. Dogs cozy up underneath them, and the beds cover them up.

## Treats

Treats are essential for almost any kind of training. It's good to use kibble in early training stages. Then move on to other high-quality, healthy treats: carrots, sweet potatoes, peanut butter, blueberries, and apples, to name just a few. You can use meat as well but be careful with bones.

There's a huge variety of commercially manufactured treats, but exercise caution. Anything that has a long shelf life probably isn't healthy for your dog—or for you.

### Chews, Toys, and Bones

Many dogs are avid chewers, so it's important to find one or more good chew varieties that will keep your dog busy for a long time. A

## BEWARE EXTRA-DURABLE CHEWS

Most people want their dog chews to be as durable and long-lasting as possible. But be careful! Very durable dog chews, which do not show signs of wear, will typically wear your dog's teeth down instead. Either the chew is giving way, or your dog's teeth are.

good chew also has health benefits, providing minerals for joints and bones and contributing to dental health.

The dizzying array of chews and chewable dog toys include:

- **Rawhide**. These are probably the most widely available and common chew. However, there are a number of possible issues, especially with imported rawhide chews. The "rawhide" is not raw but heavily processed, often with toxic chemicals. Dogs have also been known to choke on rawhides.[5]

- **Hooves and antlers**. Beef hooves in particular are very popular because they're natural and long-lasting, durable chews.

- **Learning toys**. These are toys into which treats are inserted. They're often puzzles that require your dog to figure out how to get to the goodies.

- **Tugs and ropes**. These are pretty self-explanatory. However, it's worth pointing out that they're great relationship-builders and tools for teaching your dog how to fetch/tug.

- **Rubber chews**. These are very durable but won't do damage to your dog's teeth.

- **Nylon chews**. Like rubber chews, these won't hurt your dog's teeth. They come in all different shapes and forms. Many types are bone shaped.

- **Dental and edible chews**. These are chews meant to be eaten once they've given your dog's mouth and teeth a good workout. They're usually made out of starch or other natural ingredients.

---

5. Annie Stuart, "Rawhide: Good or Bad for Your Dog?" Fetch by WebMD, last reviewed May 8, 2021, https://pets.webmd.com/dogs/rawhide-good-or-bad-for-your-dog#1.

## Your Shopping List

For a curated selection of the best products on the market, stop by mindyourpaws.com/ shop, where you'll find a handy shopping list of the items you'll need and want to get for the journey.

mindyourpaws.com/shop

## Dog Identification and Registration

Dog tags and other identification help ensure that, if your dog gets lost, its owner—you—can be contacted to retrieve your pet.

### Legal Registration

Registration requirements vary from county to county and municipality to municipality. Registration procedures also vary enormously. The best way to find out what's required in your city or county is to talk with your vet. In fact, registration, which frequently involves rabies and other vaccinations, is often done through veterinary offices.

### Microchips

Dog tags are the most common type of canine ID. But it's always possible for tags or the collars to which they're attached to fall off.

Another option would be to get a microchip implanted just under your dog's skin by a very simple surgical procedure. This is often done at the same time a dog is fixed.

Local municipalities, counties, or Humane Societies often offer free microchipping for the local community. It's worth checking out if this is true in yours.

A microchip will allow any vet, animal hospital, shelter, or pound to identify your dog and its owner. The dog is scanned and, if a microchip is found, its owner-identification data is looked up on a database.

This means your dog's microchip will only work as directed if it's been registered on a database such as the American Kennel Club's AKC Reunite. All canine microchip databases can be accessed through the Universal Pet Microchip Lookup Tool of the AAHA (American Animal Hospital Association).

A microchip isn't a GPS and can't be used to give your dog's exact location. On the other hand, a GPS—yes, you can get a GPS device for your pup—won't identify who a dog's owner is. It can also be lost, just like a dog tag, and requires batteries.

For info on microchips, visit mindyourpaws.com/book/resources.

mindyourpaws.com/
book/resources

## Dangerous Household Items

The following list is meant to bring your attention to common household hazards that could endanger your dog. It's not exhaustive. Keep an eye out and take commonsense precautions!

### ASPCA ANIMAL POISON CONTROL HOTLINE

The ASPCA (American Society for the Prevention of Cruelty to Animals) runs an animal poison control center. It should be your first port of call in any poison-related emergency.

Call: 888-426-4435

### Inside

- **Cords** are not only a chewing but a fall hazard. Make sure your dog doesn't play behind the TV, a computer, or anywhere there are a lot of cords.

- **Cleaning products** are often toxic if ingested.[6]
- **Flowers and house plants** can be poisonous, depending on the plant. You can find a complete list at mindyourpaws.com/book/resources.
- **Garbage cans and clothes hampers** are places where your pet can easily get trapped.

*Outside*

All of the following substances found around the house and garage are toxic or potentially so:

- Insecticides
- Rat poison
- Herbicides
- Antifreeze
- Mulch

*Food*

ALCOHOL

AVOCADO  CAFFEINE  COOKED BONES  CHOCOLATE

DAIRY  MOST DANGEROUS FOODS FOR DOGS  FATTY FOODS

milk

GRAPES  MUSHROOMS  ONIONS GARLIC  RAISINS CURRANTS

WALNUTS MACADAMIAS  XYLITOL

---

6. "Potentially Dangerous Items for Your Pet," FDA, last reviewed February 28, 2023, https://www.fda.gov/animal-veterinary/animal-health-literacy/potentially-dangerous-items-your-pet.

## Proper Planning

Adorable as they are, puppies are vulnerable to all sorts of dangers when they're small. Take the time to think about how to make your home safe for the new arrival *before* they show up, and you'll likely save yourself from a few minor calamities—and possibly something more serious.

# PART III:

# WELCOME HOME

Okay, crunch time. Most new dog owners are basically clueless. Fortunately, you don't have to be one of them! In this part of the book, we'll ensure that you know what to do when your puppy comes home. In particular, we'll set you up to successfully accomplish your first goal: potty training. Nervous at the new addition to your family and in need of reassurance? Don't sweat it. These tips from the trenches will ease your worries.

CHAPTER 7:

# HOW TO SURVIVE THE FIRST TWENTY-FOUR HOURS

It's exciting to bring a cute puppy home. As your dog's owner, you're looking forward to having a lot of fun with your new family member. And, of course, you're up for the work involved.

Early on, however, there will also be times when you'll think, "What did I get myself into?" You may find yourself standing in the pouring rain, while your puppy stares uncomprehendingly up at you, oblivious to the fact that you want it to go to the bathroom. Eventually, you give up and bring your dog inside, only for it to pee on the kitchen floor.

These moments are frustrating. But if you know what you're doing, they need not be a disaster. Knowing what to expect when you first get a puppy, and what your puppy should expect from you, will go a long way to getting you over the hump.

## First Steps

The potential for stickiness—both emotional and literal—begins as soon as you take possession of your new pup. The first car ride when you bring them home is an adventure, but be aware that your new puppy may have an accident or even get carsick. Bring someone with you to help. Let the puppy play outside and empty its tank before getting in the car. If the ride home is going to be a long one, plan some stops, so your puppy can stretch its legs and take additional potty breaks.

When you get your puppy home, take things nice and slow. Start by introducing the dog to the family and any other pets or animals in the house. Remember that puppies have three basic modes: food mode, play mode, and sleep mode. Rinse and repeat.

In the first few weeks, you need to focus on boundary-setting, crate and potty training, socialization/exposure, handling, and feeding. More advanced training will come later.

You may be lucky enough to get that fabled "easy" dog, who never gives you any trouble. But don't count on it. Your best approach is to hope for the best and prepare for the worst, so you're not blindsided. Accept that there will be accidents and sleepless nights listening to your puppy crying. Above all, enjoy your time with your dog.

Here's an overview of what you can expect.

## Boundary-Setting

The biggest mistake most people make is giving their cute new puppies too much freedom, too soon. Like any good relationship, take things nice and slow. Gradually introduce your pup to more of its new home, and give it time to settle in.

The same rules apply both inside and outside the house. Your puppy should be supervised or contained, so that bad habits don't start when you're not looking. Manage your dog's space appropriately. Use the baby gates, crates, and exercise pens recommended in Chapter 6: Puppy Proofing. You can attach your dog to a leash while it's in the house and even clip the other end of the leash to yourself. Control your new friend's environment as much as possible.

## There Are Three S's in Success

Properly training and raising a dog demands commitment. You will need to make some sacrifices. At the beginning of its life, your puppy will require much more of your time than it will later on. During this initial period, you're teaching your dog rules. The more diligent and consistent you are at first, the more quickly and easily you'll be able to introduce more freedom.

There are three S's in success and three S's in your successful approach to training: schedule, structure, and supervision.

## Schedule

The more tightly scheduled your time with your puppy, the more successful you'll be. Make sure your puppy gets into a regular feeding and water routine, as well as exercise, play, and crate timetables.

You want to set your dog's expectations. The more you schedule, the easier it'll be to tell when the dog needs to go to the bathroom. Since you feed and water your dog at the same time every day, your daily potty schedule will be the same as well.

We'll go further—much further!—into potty training below.

## Structure

Scheduling is about time, and structure is about space. You want to give your puppy lots of opportunity to go where they should go and zero opportunity to go where they shouldn't.

Puppies generally like structure. Although there will be an adjustment period, they want to know what your expectations and their opportunities are. Structure prevents mistakes from happening. Expectations permit puppies to set themselves up for success. Giving your pup free rein means it'll start chewing on things they're not supposed to chew on and get access to dangerous areas.

For example, don't give puppies the run of the entire house at first. Slowly introduce them to the areas of the house where they're allowed.

Section off the main area where you want your puppy to hang out. The kitchen is a great place to start. Kitchens typically have floors that are easy to clean, which helps with potty issues. There are no couches inherited from grandma or other expensively upholstered furniture that your pup might grab and chew on.

As the dog starts getting accustomed to the kitchen, you can increase its access into other areas. But do that slowly and steadily.

## Supervision

When your puppy is out of its crate or exercise pen, you should be directly supervising it. Being diligent early on will pay off in the long run.

You're looking to spot any subtle cues that your puppy needs to go to the bathroom. Keeping your eye on the dog will also prevent chewing problems, which can both save your precious furniture and keep your pup safe from hazards like cables.

Supervision also allows you to build a relationship with your dog. When your puppy is hanging out with you, you should be present for and interacting with it. During your dog's supervised free time, you're both teaching it and building a bond.

When it's time to get your work done—cooking, family time with the kids, homework, and other household tasks—utilize the dog's crate or playpen.

Most dog owners work a typical 9-to-5 job and don't have the luxury of being at home with their puppies all day. Get help! Recruit a neighbor, young or old, who can let the dog out during the day. It's not unusual for a puppy to be in its crate for eight hours at a stretch—as long as it's able to get breaks.

Given direction and attention, your dog will quickly start learning what it's allowed and not allowed to do. If you don't put that work in on the front end, you'll spend a lot more time later on correcting bad behavior that, with early training, never would have happened in the first place.

Failing to supervise your pup's early days is like putting yourself into debt. Before long, the interest will mount, and you'll need to work twice as hard to dig yourself out of a self-imposed hole.

## TOP TIPS TO JUMP-START POTTY TRAINING

Remember to take your puppy out at all these times:

AFTER:

- Feeding
- Drinking water
- Waking up from a nap
- Play
- Training sessions
- Any excitement (dogs, people, or toys)
- Being in their crate
- Waking up in the morning

BEFORE:

- Going to bed at night

## Crate Training

You might like living the Lifestyles of the Rich and InstaFamous. But dogs enjoy denning in small spaces. Puppies typically like to hide behind couches or under tables and beds. They're comfortable in smaller, charming cottages.

A crate isn't a punishment but an instinctual comfort. You should help your dog understand that its crate is a safe spot, although not a place to go to the bathroom.

Your cute puppy will begin to show its true colors during its first few nights in the crate. Expect to get up once or twice to let it out. This won't be true of all puppies, but you should be prepared. There will be some sleepless nights the first few weeks, while your puppy adjusts. But fear not! Before long, you'll resume your normal routine.

At first, bring your dog's meals into the crate, so it builds positive associations with its new den. Your puppy should both eat and sleep in the crate—the nighttime is the right time for its crate! Again, any time you can't keep your eyes on your pup, put it in its crate or exercise pen.

If you're looking for tools to help your pup get comfortable in its crate, check out mindyourpaws.com/shop for a list of my favorites.

## TEETHING TROUBLES

Puppies have a low boredom threshold and distract themselves by chewing. I strongly recommend you crate your dog until it's eighteen months old, to avoid teething and chewing disasters.

It's better to prevent mistakes from happening than to have to repair your furniture. A lot of owners who have gotten through the initial six-month teething phase think their dog is ready to be given more freedom. If you make this error, you may come home to discover your pup has decorated your couch with a new pattern called "teeth marks."

## Feeding

There's no such thing as a free lunch—especially when feeding your new dog. Mealtimes are the perfect training times.

Get your dog comfortable with a number of different feeding styles and regimens. Feed it by hand some days and combine this feeding with handling its paws and ears. Also, remember to feed your puppy in its crate to foster positive associations with its new den.

Meals are also great times to create name associations. Use your dog's name prior to giving it food. You can also start using the word "come" just before mealtimes. If you are an overachiever, you can also expect a "sit" before you put down the food bowl.

## Don't Lean on Cookie

A lot of people use cute words such as "cookie" or "treat" when feeding their dogs. This is a wasted opportunity because the word "cookie" can't be applied in other circumstances. If you use "come" or their name right before you open that special jar instead, you're teaching your dog to associate a useful command with a food reward.

# Potty and House Training

Potty and house training are two ways of saying the same thing. Whichever word you use, it begins as soon as you bring your puppy home. It's especially important to create a schedule—one of the three S's.

**PUPPY POTTY** *Log*

Your personal assistant for puppy potty training! Being a puppy parent is the most wonderful experience, except housebreaking. The key to housetraining your puppy is a consistent schedule. Log your dog's pees, poops, and meals, and Puppy Potty Log will use the data to predict a unique housetraining schedule for your pup. Remember that predictable input (food and water) = predictable output (poop and pee). Find out more at: https://potty.app.

https://potty.app

## Potty Scheduling

It takes a puppy time to get into a structured schedule. It may be a struggle to work through this at first, so early on you'll want to proactively get your dog out to go to the bathroom every hour or so, until you start seeing a pattern.

Deliberately escort it out on a leash early on. You want to walk out with the puppy to make sure it's doing the deed and see whether it does #1 or #2.

## Set Your Dog Up for Success

When young puppies poop in the house, the fault lies with their owners, who haven't created a schedule they can easily adhere to. Your pup should be on a set feeding, watering, and potty schedule. Any food your pup doesn't finish within a five-minute time span should be removed from its reach. A hungry or thirsty dog won't take more than five minutes to eat their food and drink water.

The exception comes if you have a finicky dog who picks at their food. If this describes your pup, give them ten minutes to eat. If you want to give your dog water but not fill their bladder, ice cubes are a great solution. Ice cubes also help to soothe gums that are sore from teething and give your dog something to crunch if they want it.

When your dog finishes eating, set a timer. In most cases, twenty minutes is a safe timeframe to allow food and water to pass through a dog's digestive system. After the dog finishes eating, and before the timer goes off, keep a close eye on suspicious behavior that might indicate the dog needs to go potty. If they haven't gone when the timer goes off, take them out.

Even if your dog goes right away, stay in the potty area a few more minutes, since puppies don't always empty their bladders all at once. Once outside, if your dog doesn't go potty within five to ten minutes, bring it inside and put it in its crate for fifteen to twenty minutes. Then take it back outside for another try. Keep interchanging between the crate and outside. If this happens a lot, extend the gap between giving your dog food/drink and taking them out, in small increments. Expect this to happen naturally anyway, as your pup grows.

## Rewarding and Withholding

Unless the dog successfully goes potty, do *not* allow it to roam free. The reward for going to the bathroom is free time. Let your puppy run around and play in the yard. Or take it back into the house and give it some supervised fun time.

Save treats for after you come back into the house. This way you're adding value to returning inside after playtime. Don't reward your dog with a treat when it goes potty outside. If your dog is smart enough— and, of course, it is!—it may start associating a treat with squatting but not actually going to the bathroom. Use playtime, off-leash in your backyard if it's fenced off, as a reward.

# THE MONTH PLUS ONE RULE

How long can your pet stay in its crate without fear of an accident? There's a quick rule of thumb for how long a dog can hold its bladder. It's called the "month plus one" rule.

The age of your puppy in months plus one is the maximum number of hours your puppy should be able to hold it comfortably between potty breaks.

If your puppy is three months old, adding one gives a four-hour maximum limit.

Now you see why you need to recruit backup to come in and let your dog out when you're at work.

## How Long?

Potty training usually takes a few months. Relapses, sometimes caused by changes in weather and introduction to new environments, are common. Just because your puppy is accident-free for a week or two doesn't necessarily mean it's fully potty trained.

The more consistent you are with schedule and structure, the more successful your potty training will be. Potty training is something you need to incorporate into your lifestyle for several months. The most common mistake is believing your dog's training is bulletproof after two weeks of success.

## Weather

The weather will also affect how often your dog needs—and wants—to go potty. Dogs may be afraid of going potty outside during rainy, hot, or cold weather, resulting in relapses. It's tempting to go easy on them at these times, but it's important they get used to the idea that potty is compulsory. Winter can actually be a good time to instill a solid potty habit, with few distractions in comparison with lively summer months.

## Correction

It's a common—and very wrong—practice to correct a dog after the fact by taking them to the spot where they had an accident. Some people even advocate rubbing your dog's nose in its poop. This is terrible advice that just encourages your pooch to start hiding its behavior. If you get tempted to punish your pooch after an accident, try this instead: roll up a newspaper and, as sternly as you can, bonk *yourself* on the nose. Yeah, it's not your dog's fault. They're too young to know better. It's *yours*.

Trying to correct your dog after the fact could create fear of going to the bathroom in front of you, which is something you do not want to encourage. Should you do this, you'll soon start finding poop in other rooms or behind your couch. It now becomes more difficult to catch cues that your dog needs to go to the bathroom in time to get it outside.

If you do catch your dog in the act, make an interrupter noise and then take it outside to finish. An interrupter noise is a startling sound, such as a handclap. You want to interrupt the dog in the act of going potty in the house, and then run it outside to let it finish its bathroom break.

### Paper Training and Pee Pads

If your goal is to get your dog to go to the bathroom outside, I don't recommend paper training or pee pads. But people who live in apartments several stories up may opt to use pee pads, and that's fine.

Paper or pee pads shouldn't be left out all the time. Rather, lay them down as a cue for your dog to go to the bathroom. Use the same scheduling and supervision process you would as if you were taking the dog out. Now, instead of taking it out, put paper down to let your puppy know it's time to do its business. Even better, put the pad outside in the hallway or patio, to make for an easier transition to outdoor puppy potty notifications.

## Socialization and Exposure

Many pet owners and even trainers emphasize puppy "socialization," but it's now time to retire this word, along with YOLO, metrosexual, and using "literally" before every sentence. The biggest problem with the word is that owners feel it implies that everyone your dog encounters should be able to pet it, and every other dog you encounter should be able to come up to your dog, sniff around, and play.

Could you imagine if we had this expectation with children?! You don't want a random stranger running up to your child and start rubbing their head and petting their belly. You shouldn't put this kind of expectation on your dog, either.

The most important thing you're doing with exposure training is teaching your dog how to move through the world without fear, on the one hand, and with good manners, on the other. People think they are "socializing" their dog if they take it to a dog park or, to use an apt expression, the prison yard. You need to be careful, because such random, scattershot interactions could cause fear, anxiety, and phobias later in your dog's life.

True confessions time. Although the word "socialization" is overused and can be confusing, it's so common that it's hard to avoid completely. It's already and will continue to come up in this manual.

Also, taking precautions against single-event learning is particularly important in the context of exposure, so, before diving in more deeply, it's worth repeating what was said on this subject earlier.

## Sights and Sounds

In exposing your puppy to the sights and sounds it's bound to encounter, you want to create positive associations. You want to expose it to bikes, scooters, cars, traffic, lawn mowers, vacuum cleaners, and sirens by taking it to various environments slowly and carefully. Start around your house in your back and front yards. Then move down the block to your neighbors' yards and the immediate neighborhood, getting it comfortable in those situations.

Pace your pup carefully and build up a variety of interactions. Take your puppy to the local hardware store and coffee shop. Include restaurant patios where dogs are allowed.

Brewpubs are great, but probably not the best places to take a twelve-week-old puppy. Scale up to such busier and more highly trafficked areas over time. Puppies are attention magnets. But take it slowly. Don't move faster than your dog allows.

Bring lots of treats as your dog gets used to different noises and sounds. These will help the dog relax.

It may take a few days or weeks to work through fearful situations. Continue making your dog more comfortable in these before adding on.

## People

Every dog should be an EOC—equal opportunity canine. It's important to expose your dog to people of different ages, genders, and races, as well as to people who dress differently and wear accessories such as hats and glasses.

Dogs will be leery of types of people they haven't seen before. It's critical that you help your puppy get over that. The more variety, the better.

Structure—one of the three S's—is, as always, essential. Have a game plan. As much as possible, structure introductions and new interactions. The key is creating as many positive associations as possible, although this does not mean allowing little Susie to tug your dog's ear, or Hawaiian shirt man to kiss your dog on the face. Plan ahead whenever you can to control your pup's environment. The rule I have is people don't meet puppies, puppies meet people. Let your dog control proximity and pace; this will lead to a confident and comfortable pup.

## Other Dogs

Structure is equally important when exposing your puppy to other dogs. The first dogs your puppy should meet should be friendly neighborhood dogs or the dogs of friends or family.

Structure a little playtime with one other dog—not two or three or five. This could be done off-leash in your or a friend's backyard. You want to minimize the number of variables involved.

Make sure your puppy is exposed to as many good experiences as possible early on. Then a single bad interaction is far less likely do long-term harm.

If you're walking your dog and someone asks if their dog can say hello to yours, ask, "Is your dog okay with other dogs?" If the answer isn't an immediate "Absolutely," keep moving. The early stage isn't a time to roll the dice. You want to make sure that both you and the other dog's owner are confident that it can be trusted. If not, it's better to move on than risk a bad experience.

Use your best judgment. If someone's dog seems aggressive or out of control, don't let your dog interact with it. Not even if the owner says, "Oh, yeah, my dog is friendly."

## DOG PARKS

I'm not opposed to dog parks. I actually take my dogs to enjoy the space offered by my tax dollars. But there are better options for young puppies. The prison yard isn't a place to learn social norms. Worse, there's no way of knowing whether other dogs are properly vaccinated. Anything might happen, and it's critical not to put your dog at risk. Once your puppy has built up a treasure chest of good experiences, single-event, fear-based learning is less likely.

## Surfaces and Textures

Depending where you live, you may need to familiarize your dog with different types of terrain and weather conditions. For example, it may have never seen snow or grass before.

The same goes for household surfaces. Expose your puppy to as many as possible to prevent phobias from occurring later. Concrete, rugs, hardwood, stairs, hallways—the last thing you need is an otherwise adult dog with a phobia of stairs. What happens if you decide to replace your carpet with hardwood floors? Will your dog suddenly start playing The Floor is Lava every time it walks into your living room?

Early on, most puppies are highly adaptable. If you expose them to a lot of different situations while they're young, you can prevent issues from taking hold when they encounter something unfamiliar. The goal is getting a neutral response, one that's neither overly excitable nor fearful.

## Handling

Handling doesn't just mean petting your dog. Early on, get your dog used to things like having its paws, ears, and belly touched. Lay it on its back, play with its ears, open its mouth, and handle its entire body.

This is easy to do with a young puppy and a lot of fun. It's also a critical step to getting your dog ready for more advanced training. It will need these skills when you take it to the groomer or the vet.

Again, structure the handling. At first, only allow one person to handle the dog, and only for short periods of time. Gradually build up to letting other people, such as family members, neighbors, and friends, play with your pup.

# CHAPTER 8:

# TIPS FROM THE TRENCHES

If you've ever sat at the kitchen table staring at a mounting selection of bills, you know how it feels to be in debt. It's a long, hard slog to get back to the black.

The same principle applies to your pup's behavior. If you let them develop bad habits early on, you'll be operating at a disadvantage when you do start to train them. Why do that to yourself?

This chapter is the puppy training equivalent of a financial advisor. It will point out things many people do with new puppies and later regret. These actions may seem cute at first but are detrimental when it comes time for real training.

## Family Brainstorm Session

Whatever you want to accomplish, you'll need to make sure everyone in the household is on the same page. A big part of this requires setting rules that everyone in the house will follow and priming every family member to use the same cue words and commands.

mindyourpaws.com/guides

Yes, that's right. To train your dog, you'll also need to train the owners. Everyone in your home needs to be clear with your dog about expectations and boundaries. Clear expectations lead to success.

But how do you get family members to agree? Simple—by calling a family meeting to discuss everyone's goals. Lay everything out on the table and talk about what's important to each of you. Then the whole family can agree on the rules.

Discuss why each rule is important. For example: "We don't want the dog jumping on people when they come in the door. It may be cute now, but it'll stop being cute very soon."

"You want to pet the dog when you come home from school. But make sure the dog sits nicely before you pet it. We want a well-trained dog that follows commands."

Obviously, this process holds potential for conflict, between parents and kids or between spouses. Don't let it turn into a wrestling match. Instead, give each family member time to make their case. Some situations will be clear-cut, whereas others may allow for and require compromise.

## Hiding Things

It's tempting to hide away the things you don't want your dog to chew, such as shoes, mail, and couches. Unless you plan on moving all your furniture into the basement, however, there's another way. It's much better to keep these things in the open and train your dog to stay away from them. This includes garbage cans, laundry baskets, paperwork, and bathroom and kitchen towels.

The key, as always, is structure, schedule, and supervision. You're not going to conquer the world all at once. Work one item at a time. Teach your dog to stay away from one object—then another, and another. These are not its toys.

## Nips

Puppies are impossibly cute. Even when they're nipping you. It's easy to say, "Oh, the dog isn't biting. It's mouthing. I like it when it does that. It's giving me kisses."

Excusing early cuteness, however, may lead you to reinforce a bad behavior. Will it be cute when your pup starts nipping guests or other family members, especially children? If you encourage it, you're setting yourself up for trouble. Nipping can turn into biting and, like a stone rolling down a hill, will be much harder to stop once it gets started.

## Greeting Guests

When the doorbell rings, many new owners excitedly ask their puppies, "Who's at the door? Who's here!?" This only arouses the dog and leads to bad habits, such as rushing at the door and jumping on guests. Encouraging this behavior, your pup might also escape into the street and compromise its safety.

You want to make sure you're teaching your dog how to calmly invite guests into the house. We'll talk about this in greater depth when we discuss place or spot training in Chapter 13.

For the time being, know that it's best not to make a big deal out of someone coming to your door. Visitors are commonplace and nothing to get overly excited about.

## Too Much Excitement Coming Home

The above principle goes double for not making a fuss when you come home from work, shopping, or any other excursion. Being excessively enthusiastic when you come home can cause issues such as excited peeing and separation anxiety.

Play it cool when you first come home. Then get your dog outside. Save the excitement and energy for playtime.

Your dog will be naturally happy to see you, there's no need to amplify the excitement. You're probably also excited to see your new puppy. But think about what they need to grow up healthy and emotionally balanced. I know it's hard, but restrain yourself.

## Letting Your Puppy Jump On People

Just like pups who nip, pups who jump up seem cute. Who doesn't like being assaulted by adorable balls of fluff? Unfortunately, encouraging this behavior only leads to trouble later, when the dogs are bigger and harder to control.

Manners are important, even when you're not in public, and not everyone you meet is going to be a dog person. Keep your puppy down, no matter how cute you think it is. Work your sit and place or spot commands, which we'll go over in Chapter 13.

You can also use a leash to manage this behavior. As we've discussed, it's often a good idea to keep your new puppy on leash even inside the house.

## ARE SMALL DOGS HARDER TO TRAIN?

No, smaller dogs aren't fundamentally harder to train than large ones, no matter what a lot of people may think.

But smaller dogs often get away with more. Their owners are less concerned with fixing bad behaviors because they figure those behaviors probably won't become a liability. You're less likely to let your Doberman puppy jump on people than your Chihuahua. Side note: Have you ever met the Chihuahua from hell? Now you have an idea why.

If you create the same expectations with smaller dogs as you would for a larger breed, they will become just as well trained and well behaved as their bigger cousins. It's up to you to make and manage those expectations.

## Feeding from the Table

This one should be a no-brainer. But clearly dogs get fed from the table all the time.

If you don't want your dog to hover around whenever you're eating—and believe me, you don't—don't feed it from the table.

Grandma may be easily seduced into dropping treats on the floor, but she needs to exercise some self-control!

If you want to give your dog some table scraps, put them in its dog bowl during its dinner time. As always, mealtimes are great training times. Have your dog first follow a command, so that putting table scraps in its dinner bowl becomes a reward for a behavior.

## Rushing to the Crate When Your Dog Whines

When confined alone in an unfamiliar location, puppies often get very upset. Their every puppy instinct tells them to cry out for help. Hence, many dogs make a lot of noise when they are first crated.

Your puppy is a social animal and wants to be with you, so it will start whining to attract your attention. If you rush to the crate and let your dog out as soon as it starts whining, it will learn that the way to get out of its crate is to whine. Don't reinforce the unwanted behavior.

As long as all the dog's needs have been met, you've already exercised your dog and taken it out to go to the bathroom, it shouldn't need to come out of the crate until you're ready to let it out.

## Repeating Commands

We'll be talking about naming and giving commands shortly. A lot of people get in the bad habit of repeating commands until their dog listens, like telling a naughty schoolchild to concentrate.

Instead, get in the habit of using teachable moments to fix your dog's behavior. Take the time to teach your dog a specific behavior *before* you start giving them verbal commands and expecting them to perform.

## Furniture

Should your dog be allowed on the furniture? As a parent, you may be completely against the idea. But your kids may want their puppy to cuddle and even sleep on the bed with them.

One often-effective solution is to implement an "invitation only" policy. The assumption is that the dog isn't just allowed to get on the furniture whenever it likes. When guests come over and sit on the couch, you don't want your pet vaulting into their laps.

One compromise, therefore, might be that if you want the dog to come on the couch and cuddle—let's say you want to watch *Die Hard* for the 313th time—you can invite them up and hang out. When you want it to get off, it needs to respect that command.

What happens if someone else in the family objects because they don't want the dog shedding on the couch? Okay, then. It's time for a new clause. Whenever the dog comes on the couch, it must lie on a blanket.

Tweaks like these turn conflict between family members into win-win scenarios. This outcome is a win for the dog as well, especially if it likes *Die Hard*. It can jump on the couch when someone lays down a blanket and invites it up, but it can't just get on the couch whenever it wants.

There are lots of ways to come up with compromises that allow all parties to win. Work with your family members to establish ground rules and get everyone on the same page.

# PART IV:

# TRAINING FOUNDATIONS

Now that you've picked your pup and begun the process of bonding with your new bestest buddy, you'll want to make sure they don't embarrass you in front of the neighbors. You might even pick up some tips you can apply to your spouse or your kids. This part of the book is packed with nuts and bolts info about basic canine learning principles and how to apply them—a liberal helping of practicality with a sprinkling of theory. The material in this part of the book is your CliffsNotes to understanding the killer combination of love and bribery that will bring the best out of your dog and allow them to express their full pupbilities.

## CHAPTER 9:

# LEARNING PRINCIPLES

Geek alert! Some puppy parents are interested in the *why* behind the *how*. Like engineers who enjoy rolling their sleeves up and tinkering with an engine, they want to understand what makes their dog tick.

If you're not in this group, feel free to skip this chapter and move on to the next. You won't miss anything essential. If you *are* in this group, stick around. You'll learn the basic principles of dog training. Even better, understanding the mechanics will help you to empathize with your dog the next time they do something that seems completely outside the box—or outside the crate.

If you're on the fence, join us for the ride. You'll probably find this information helpful when it comes to the nuts and bolts of training your dog. If nothing else, you'll pick up some fun facts you can share at cocktail parties.

## Primary and Secondary Reinforcers

The two most important learning principles are called classical and operant conditioning—nothing to do with types of music. Basically, conditioning is how all animals, including dogs and humans, learn.

Before we dive into classical and operant conditioning, however, let's briefly introduce a concept called reinforcers. Reinforcers come in two types: primary and secondary.

**Primary reinforcers** are basic biological drives: food, drink, and anything else that aids survival. **Secondary reinforcers** are backups that act in tandem with biological necessities: they drive behavior when they are linked to primary reinforcers.

If a dog sits when you give the command "sit," you reinforce the behavior by giving it some food. Food is a primary reinforcer. After giving it the food, you might say, "Good dog!" When repeated consistently, those words of praise become a secondary reinforcer.

Gradually, you can eliminate the primary reinforcer, food, and use just the secondary reinforcer, "Good dog!" when your pet sits on command.

A lot of human behavior is rewarded by secondary reinforcers such as compliments or currency. Money may not buy happiness, but it can buy lunch.

For dogs, secondary reinforcers might include social praise, freedom, play time, or a toy. Think of these secondary reinforcers as canine currency, which can become as powerful as primary reinforcers.

## Classical Conditioning

Classical conditioning is a process of learning by association. You link your dog's innate reflexes to react to subtle signals. Over time, your dog learns to associate the signal with the event. Mastering the concepts behind classical conditioning will help you understand how your dog understands, relates to, and interprets information.

This form of learning is also known as Pavlovian or associative learning. Ivan Pavlov was a Russian physiologist. Realizing that dogs automatically or involuntarily salivated when presented with food—a primary reinforcer—he trained his dogs to associate the ringing of a bell—a secondary reinforcer—with the appearance or presentation of food. Eventually, he was able to make the dogs salivate by just ringing a bell. A similar concept is at work in school lunch halls around the country.

## Pavlov's Principles of Classical Conditioning

- The dogs' natural salivation in response to seeing or smelling their food was their **unconditioned response.**
- The sight or smell of the food itself created an **unconditioned stimulus** or **primary reinforcer.** Food, which is necessary for survival, caused an involuntary, biological response the dog couldn't control.
- The ringing of the bell represented a **conditioned stimulus**, which previously had no association with food.
- The dog's salivation in response to the ringing of the bell was a **conditioned response** driven by a **secondary reinforcer**—even when no food was present. There's no inherent relationship between food and a bell. Pavlov's dogs salivated at the ringing of a bell because they learned to associate it with the arrival of food.

### In Practice

Here's a preview of coming attractions, explaining how you will use classical conditioning to train your dog. In classical conditioning, you associate value with a cue or marker.

When your dog obeys a command such as "sit," you first "mark" (for instance, by using a clicker, or words such as "free," "bingo," or "release"). Then, you give the dog some canine currency, such as physical touch, verbal praise, or food. In Chapter 11, we'll explain how to choose a good marker word.

When you do this, you pair an otherwise neutral stimulus with an involuntary behavior.

## Operant Conditioning

In operant conditioning, animals associate their behavior with consequences. You can link your dog's good behavior to positive rewards like a treat, a scratch behind the ears, or a trip to Vegas with a suitcase full of cash. Okay, maybe that's for me!

Operant conditioning is primarily associated with the work of American psychologist B. F. Skinner. Skinner studied and observed behaviors, as opposed to internal states. He believed that classical conditioning was too simplistic.

Skinner is famous for creating what he called a Skinner Box, which he used to conduct experiments. Iconic images such as rats touching a lever to release food and mice moving through mazes stem from Skinner's work.

Before diving into the details of operant conditioning, here's a quick overview of the differences between it and classical conditioning:

• Classical conditioning links a **neutral stimulus**—ringing of a bell—with an **involuntary response**—salivation.

• Operant conditioning links a **voluntary behavior,** such as sitting politely, with a **consequence**, such as receiving a treat. Operant conditioning pairs a secondary reinforcer—also known as a discriminative stimulus—with a learned behavior.

CLASSICAL CONDITIONING
ASSOCIATE AN INVOLUNTARY
RESPONSE AND A STIMULUS

OPERANT CONDITIONING
ASSOCIATE VOLUNTARY BEHAVIOR
AND A CONSEQUENCE

## The A, B, C's

The fundamental principle of operant conditioning is A, B, C: Antecedent—Behavior—Consequence.

- **Antecedent:** This refers to whatever comes before the behavior— the stimulus. It might be any kind of cue. A mailman, a tennis ball, a front door, a skateboarder.
- **Behavior:** The behavior is your dog's response to the antecedent. The dog is happy, gets excited, fetches the ball, or sits nicely.
- **Consequence:** The consequence is what happens when your dog performs the behavior. Does it get a reward to increase that behavior, or a punishment to decrease it?

## Reinforcement and Punishment

Operant conditioning uses both reinforcement and punishment. If you master this very effective psychology technique, you can teach a dog—or other family members—to reliably perform any tasks. Stay with us on this one. It sounds much more complicated than it is!

Both reinforcement and punishment come in two forms: positive and negative. Taken together, the four types of operant conditioning make a quadrant:

| | |
|---|---|
| Positive Reinforcement (+R) | Positive Punishment (+P) |
| Negative Reinforcement (-R) | Negative Punishment (-P) |

**Positive reinforcement** (+R) means the addition of a reward, such as a treat. If your dog gets a treat when it sits on command, it will be more likely to repeat this behavior.

**Negative reinforcement** (-R) happens when your dog's behavior causes something uncomfortable to be removed. For instance, if you want your dog, which is lying down, to sit up, you'll pull the dog's leash to an upward position, tightening the collar and creating minor discomfort. When the dog sits, the leash gives slack, and the discomfort goes away.

**Positive punishment** (+P) means the addition ("positive") of a consequence. If your dog barks and you use a squirt bottle with water, or a noise interrupter, you've introduced an aversive in order to teach them not to make so much fuss or something unpleasant will happen.

**Negative punishment** (-P) is the removal of something good. If your dog jumps on you and you step back or turn your back, removing yourself and your attention, it may associate that loss with that particular action. Again, it will be less likely to repeat it in the future.

## "POSITIVE" AND "NEGATIVE"

It's important to understand that, in operant conditioning, positive and negative do **not** equate to "good" and "bad." Positive means *adding* something. Negative means *removing* or *withdrawing* something.

## A Balanced Approach

Operant conditioning helps your dog understand that actions have consequences. Your pet will learn to moderate its behavior based on what happens after its actions. If its behavior comes with a perceived reward, it will be repeated. If there is no reward, or if it doesn't enjoy the consequences, it's less likely to repeat the behavior.

Some dog trainers and owners believe more in rewards. Some believe more in punishment. However, these aren't really different approaches. They should complement each other. What's most effective is a balanced approach that uses every tool at your disposal: positive and negative reinforcement and punishment.

The more information you provide to your dog, the easier it will become to direct it to your desired behavior. It's similar to playing the hot/cold game with a child. Reinforcement tells your dog that it is "hot" and should do more of whatever it's doing. Punishment tells it that it's cold and should moderate its behavior.

All quadrants work together, giving your dog as much information as possible to guide it toward your behavioral goals. Yes, some of this is controversial. It's important to keep in mind that positive and negative reinforcements and punishments will be different for individual dogs. Each dog has different likes and dislikes, just like you do. We'll discuss this more in upcoming chapters.

## NO PRIZES FOR PARTICIPATION

We are not in the business of giving prizes for participation, we want a winning pup. Don't forget that you are constantly shaping your dog's behavior. Every tug on the leash, every treat given or withheld, every scratch behind the ears or removal of your presence tells your dog what you want them to do more or less of.

At any given moment, you'll be accessing different corners of the quadrant. Don't get caught up in analysis paralysis. Do your best and recognize it will take a little trial and error to discover what works best. Use this framework as a way of tracking what you do and its impact on your dog's behavior.

## Reinforcement Schedule

A reinforcement schedule is a rule or set of rules that state when and how often a behavior will be reinforced:

- **Continuous reinforcement:** where the behavior is reinforced every single time it occurs.
- **Partial reinforcement:** once your dog is consistently giving you a desired response, you will want to switch from continuous reinforcement to a partial reinforcement schedule. There are three partial reinforcement schedules:
  - *Fixed ratio schedule:* the response is reinforced only after every set number of responses. For instance, every third time your dog sits, they receive a reward.
  - *Fixed interval schedule:* the response is reinforced after a specific amount of time has elapsed. For instance, you could use a fixed interval schedule for the "down stay" command. If your dog stays down for three minutes, it gets a reward. After another three minutes, it gets another reward. And so on.
  - *Variable interval schedule:* the reward is given after an unpredictable randomized amount of time, or an unpredictable number of responses, have passed.

## Relativity

No, we're not talking about Einstein here. When considering reinforcement and punishment, keep in mind that rewards and consequences are relative. A punishment for one dog might be a reward for another. The key is finding out what drives your dog, rather than what you *think* drives it. I call this finding your dog's love language.

Here's an example. You may have heard that spraying water from a spray bottle is a great way to correct a dog. For some, that may be the case. But water-loving dogs, such as Labs, will probably enjoy getting sprayed with water as much as toddlers in a paddling pool.

Rewards and punishments, like video game characters, also come in different levels. If you're in the backyard teaching your puppy to "come," kibble will probably be enough of a reward at first. Your backyard is a relatively controlled, managed environment, with limited distractions.

However, if you're trying to teach your puppy to "come" in your front yard or a park, with many more distractions, you'll probably need to increase the value of the reward you provide.

The same is true for consequences. There's a consequence for jumping on the couch, and another consequence for trying to bite you.

Like an overenthusiastic puppy, we've dived quite a way down the rabbit hole in this chapter. But, hopefully like that puppy, we're going to pull out before we go too far and get completely lost.

We could talk about behavioral extinction, learned irrelevance, or the Premack Principle, but your eyes would probably glaze over. If you like technical information, you can find those sections at mindyourpaws.com/learning-principles.

For everyone else, it's time to move on to training methods.

mindyourpaws.com/
learning-principles

# CHAPTER 10:
# TRAINING METHODS

The last chapter on training principles was about perfect-world scenarios. What works in the lab or on paper doesn't always work on the Lab in the real world. When you're working with a dog, adjustments often have to be made, and factors such as human error taken into account. Yes, you will make mistakes. Understanding the theory behind various different training methods will help you make needed adjustments.

The training methods introduced in this chapter are solid and time-tested. I use them daily to successfully train hundreds of dogs (and their owners!). In Part VI of this book, Paws to the Pavement, you'll learn how to apply the methods described here to train your dog to exhibit specific behaviors.

Effective training methods utilize and leverage your dog's natural reactions. You want to get inside your dog's mind and learn how to prompt it, giving it hints about what you're looking for. As you train your dog, you will start changing its thinking from an entitlement attitude to one of accountability.

Positive reinforcement is the cornerstone of dog training. That doesn't mean constantly showering your dog with praise and treats. Positive reinforcement should teach your dog that nothing in life is free. If they want something, they have to work for it.

# How Dogs Learn

Just like people, every dog learns differently. Some people are visual learners, others are verbal learners. Different training styles or methods may work better with different dogs, or even when teaching the same dog two different tasks. For optimum results, load your toolbox with a variety of options.

Confusion about what actually motivates your dog makes for ineffective training. You've got to get inside your dog's head and understand what they truly value! As mentioned in the previous chapter, you can think of this as your dog's love language. When you communicate with them in a way they understand, they will respond as well as possible.

The different training methods are the tools in your toolbox. The three most important—the primary training styles—are marker, lure, and target training. After these come molding and capturing techniques.

## PUPPY SEE, PUPPY DO

People communicate verbally, but your dog doesn't understand your spoken language. Dogs communicate with body language. While you're training your dog, it's reading your body language more than you probably realize.

In humans, the sense of sight trumps the sense of hearing. Try saying "touch your nose" to a child while simultaneously touching your ear. The chances are, they'll copy what they see you do, not what you tell them to do. A similar principle is at work for dogs.

This is why you shouldn't start training your dog with verbal commands. Those come later. Trust me, it's more important to *teach* the behavior before you *name* the behavior.

When you train your dog, you're manipulating them as you would manipulate a steering wheel. Often, you'll use food and other lures to position your dog the way you intend, creating behaviors that are repeatable and can be recreated predictably. That doesn't happen verbally, at least not at first.

## Marker Training

Marker training is the ground-level application of operant conditioning. This will be the foundation of your communication with your dog. You start by letting your dog know it has done something correct by making a sound—a "mark" followed by a treat—a "reward." Mark the desired behavior as soon as it happens.

Let's get really clear. Marker words are not commands, like "sit" or "come." They're sounds or cues that mark your approval of what your dog has just done.

## Clicker Training

Another option when training is to utilize something called a clicker. The clicker produces a clear, consistent, easily repeatable noise. Some people find it difficult to maintain the same tone when giving their dog verbal cues, and prefer to use clickers. They're generally a good solution. The only problem may be that it's not convenient to carry one around with you all the time.

## Consequences

As well as teaching your dog what to do, marker training is also used to teach your dog what you *don't* want it to do. When the dog is doing something wrong, use a consistent anti cue—a word like "no" or "off." Just as pro cues are followed by rewards, anti cues are followed by consequences.

## Lure Training

Lure training is like putting a carrot in front of a donkey to persuade it to move in a desired direction. Alternatively, you can think of it as luring a fish with a worm on a hook. A lure is like a magnet that attracts your dog to do what you want it to do. Lure training and marker training are the two most fundamental methods you'll use when teaching your dog new commands.

Lure training makes learning enjoyable for both you and your pet. It's a great way to bond and a good method for new owners just beginning to train their dogs.

Commonly, lure training uses food and your dog's nose to manipulate it into different positions. These positions include "sit," "down," "between," "figure eight," "spin," "turn," and "heel." The list is endless. In addition to food, toys such as a ball or games such as tug can also be used as lures.

## Targeting

Target training involves teaching your dog to touch a designated part of its body to a specific location, such as a pole, a spot on the wall, the palm of your hand, or almost anything else you choose. Targets are versatile training tools for animals, as they easily learn to touch a target to receive a click or other mark, followed by a treat.

The most common body part used in targeting is your dog's nose. However, you can teach your dog to touch a target with other parts of its body, such as their ear, shoulder, paw, or even tail. Targeting is fun to teach and a great way for dogs to learn useful behaviors, such as how to go to their spot or bed, close a door, retrieve objects, ring a bell to go outside, and turn on lights.

## Molding

Molding is physically positioning your dog, for example, by pushing down on your dog's butt to get it to sit. This type of training is usually best employed during the first six months of your puppy's life. Also, you'll want to use a minimum amount of physical assistance or force.

While this is a great tool to have in your training toolbox, it shouldn't be your primary approach. Molding is more of a secondary technique than a default training approach. Dogs, like teenagers, have a high opposition reflex—an instinctive tendency to resist pressure and retain balance. When you put your hand on your dog's backside, it will want to push against you.

Molding is like duct tape. It can be super-useful in certain situations, but it doesn't produce results as consistently as other techniques, nor is it as broadly applicable.

## Capturing

Capturing is reinforcing behaviors your dog does naturally. Successfully performing capturing requires previous marker training and patience.

Let's say you're hanging out in front of Netflix and want your dog to settle down. You wait until the dog lies down on its own, then mark and reward that activity. What you're doing is "capturing" and reinforcing a behavior the dog has already performed of its own accord.

### APPLYING CAPTURING

The most common behavior you may choose to capture is your dog signaling that it wants to go out. Let's say you're sitting somewhere in your house and your dog paws at a door. When you mark the behavior with a "yes" or "good," and then let your dog out, you're capturing and rewarding that behavior. Your dog is also rewarded, because you allow it to go outside and relieve itself.

Keep an eye on your pet as it goes about its business. As soon as it performs a behavior you're trying to teach it, sound your clicker or say your marker word, then give it a reward. Do this immediately, with as short a gap as possible between behavior and marker. This will reinforce the connection between the behavior and treats.

Capturing is another good supplement to your training tools, but typically not enough on its own.

## Advanced Training Techniques

Just like the last chapter, it would be possible to expand much further on this subject. There are several more advanced techniques you could use to train your dog. The question is, do you really need them? If you're bringing your first puppy home, you'll have plenty on your mind without trying to absorb more than you need.

If you'd like to know more, perhaps because you're already skilled in the basics or you're interested in exploring the subject more thoroughly, check out mindyourpaws.com/dog-training-methods. We've got a section covering complex techniques such as counterconditioning, systemic desensitization, and flooding—not the type where your puppy won't stop going to the bathroom inside.

Now, let's move on from training principles and techniques to puppies themselves. As you plan to bring a new family member into your home, what do you need to know? Let's line your expectations up with reality.

mindyourpaws.com/
dog-training-methods

**PART V:**

# THE HEADS-(P)UP

If there's one thing you should be aware of before you start training your pup, it's that the journey won't be a smooth one. In fact, it'll likely be bumpier than riding a quad bike across a sand dune. That's not only okay, it's totally normal. Like small humans, small dogs are unpredictable, easily distracted, and often maddening. But the effort is all worth it in the end.

Don't treat training as a military exercise. Everything you want to do with your dog is relationship based, and there's no point ruining the relationship just to make a point. The trusting bond that you form with your dog is the ultimate reward for all your hard work. This part of the book will set you up to be a pawrent who trains the right way.

# CHAPTER 11:
# TRAINING GUIDELINES

When you first get a puppy, trying to take on too much training is only going to set you both up for failure. But once you've done some potty training and established some structure, your puppy will finally be settling in.

Now—typically at twelve weeks and up—is a good time to start working on more advanced, formal obedience training. With a slightly older dog, you've got a little more Play-Doh to mold their mind with.

It really helps to understand the on-the-ground foundations of training before getting started. Next up, a helpful overview of how training works before you move into teaching specific commands.

## Progress, Not Perfection

Training isn't linear because learning isn't linear. Your dog will catch on to some things easily—to others, not so much.

Many people worry about getting their dog to do everything perfectly right off the bat. Instead, look for and celebrate little wins. You wouldn't expect your kid to excel at science, art, and sports all at once. Cut your dog a little slack and the training experience will be more relaxed and rewarding for everyone involved.

Making sure you're working toward good habits every day will yield better results than doing something really well today and not doing it at all the following week.

## TRAINING TRUMPS EXPECTATION

Have you ever struggled to meet the expectations of a demanding boss or teacher? What happened? You probably felt stressed as hell. And did you match those expectations, or did you feel like you were constantly failing?

The ancient Greek poet Archilochus expressed this principle best when he said, "We don't rise to the level of our expectation. We fall to our level of training." Or, as Tony Robbins puts it, "Repetition is the mother of skill."

In other words, we achieve what we're capable of achieving, not what others demand of us. You won't speed up your dog's progress by expecting it to follow six commands before breakfast when it's twelve weeks old. You'll only create a miserable experience for you and your pup alike.

In the early stages of training, aim to create a lot of "messy," rather than perfect, behaviors. Don't just work on "sit" for eight weeks. Test out your pup by trying out lots of different commands. Look for progress and a desire to learn, not for the ability to follow one command beautifully.

## Relationship-Based Training

The most important aspect of training is to build mutual respect and communication between you and your dog. You're building a relationship that can't be outsourced. That's why you got a dog in the first place, right?

People often forget that in order for their dog to live the best life possible, it needs to be able to coexist with them and fit into their life. If your dog doesn't know how to behave in the presence of guests, and your solution is putting it in a separate room when you have people over, that's not fair to either of you.

There's a famous *New Yorker* cartoon depicting a drowning man, with his dog watching from the bank of the river. The caption reads, "Lassie, get help." In the second panel, the dog is lying on a psychiatrist's couch. It's funny, but too many dog owners actually do contribute to their pets' negative emotional states.

Don't sweep issues under the rug, preventing your dog from being a part of your and your family's life. This may mean using consequences and aversives as well as rewards.

If your dog can't walk down the street and your solution is not to walk the dog, but instead fence in your backyard, that hurts both you and your dog. A much better solution is simply to work with the dog, so it learns to walk beside you.

You can pay for someone to come and walk your dog or clean up its poop. You can pay to send your dog away to be trained. But you can't pay somebody to build your relationship with your dog. That you have to do yourself.

## Consistency

Dogs always look for the loophole, so be as consistent as you can with your training. If you remember what you want to reinforce in the long term, your dog will start to display predictable behavior.

Yes, sometimes you don't have a lot of time. But beware of using your busyness as an excuse for poor habits. When you come home from work, for example, make sure your dog is settled when you let it out of the crate. You may be excited, but you need to maintain composure so that your dog behaves with you the way you would expect it to behave with others.

When you're working on leash-walking, don't let being in a hurry

**MONEY BUYS A DOG, ONLY LOVE WAGS ITS TAIL**

prevent you from making sure your dog doesn't pull. Take a few moments to fix the issue. This may cut the distance of your walk, but it will pay off in terms of your long-term goals.

## Rewarding Attitude over Behavior

Focus on rewarding attitude over behavior. You want to get your puppy excited to learn.

Some days the training may run as smoothly as the 1985 Chicago Bears. Others, it may resemble the 2017 Cleveland Browns. As long as your dog is trying and the two of you are communicating, you're laying the right foundations.

When your dog is twelve weeks old, don't expect it to walk flawlessly on a leash. Don't worry about your dog sitting and staying absolutely put when someone walks in your door.

Reward a willingness to learn. You'll know your dog is displaying the right attitude if it's happy, wants to please you, and is looking for direction. That means it's ready and able to be trained.

## Patience

Amazon may offer one-hour delivery service but your puppy will take their own sweet time. Don't rush them. Slow down and let them smell the roses.

You need to be patient and give dogs downtime, especially during training. Even when we humans learn something, we need to let the lessons settle, so we can comprehend what we've learned.

Early on, slowing it down a little bit is very helpful. Give your dog time to learn at its own pace.

## School Supplies

Just like a kid going to school for the first time, your dog will need a few supplies to excel. For a full list of recommended items, visit www. mindyourpaws.com/shop, although you may have already purchased these as we discussed them in Chapter 6: Puppy Proofing.

You'll also want to keep dog kibble and tasty treats convenient, so you can reward your dog as soon as it follows a command.

mindyourpaws.com/shop

## Relativity: Rewards and Consequences

Rewards and consequences are not absolute. They're relative to one another. Find out your dog's value system and base your training on what motivates them. This may take some experimentation.

At one end of the spectrum is under-motivation, where your dog doesn't seem that excited by the rewards you offer. At the other end of the spectrum is over-motivation. Sometimes, a dog may be so

## MAKE IT A DINNER DATE

Or a breakfast or lunch date. Use your dog's mealtime (or just before mealtime) as currency. A solid value proposition, like a meal, makes it much easier to get your dog to do what you want.

Most people are afraid of their dog missing a meal or two. But one of the great things about dogs is they don't have an image to uphold. They have no desire to be featured on the cover of *Cosmopolitan*.

If a dog is hungry, it will eat. If not, food will lose its value as a motivator. If your dog is not hungry enough to work, it's not hungry enough to eat. A motivated dog is a dog you can train.

Of course, this is true only if your dog has a healthy food drive and no other relevant issues or concerns.

motivated by a food or toy reward that it gets over-amped, making it difficult to train. If your dog has an extreme food drive, you may not be able to use food as a reward. If it's extremely driven by a ball or toy, that may not be what you want to motivate it with.

Sometimes motivators can compete with one another. You may be holding a treat in your hand at the same time your dog sees a squirrel. Even if your dog loves treats, you may struggle to compete with the chance of chasing a squirrel.

Circumstances determine perception. Einstein famously said: "Put your hand on a hot stove for a minute, and it seems like an hour. Sit with a pretty girl for an hour, and it seems like a minute. That's relativity." It's the same for your dog, and a fundamental principle you should be aware of during training.

## Other Currencies

There are hundreds of currencies in the world, and food isn't the only currency you can use to reward your dog. There's physical touch, verbal praise, social praise, play, toys—and the "fun you" or happy owner.

We'd all like a reward every time we do something, but if that happened we would soon get complacent. That chocolate cake tastes so much better as an occasional treat than as a breakfast staple.

You don't have to give your dog a treat every time you want to reward it. Use other currencies to give yourself more variety. This way you'll always have ready ways of rewarding the behavior you want to reinforce.

Verbal praise simply involves giving your pet an enthusiastic "good dog." Social praise is when you allow your dog to play with you or other dogs. Letting people pet your dog out in public is also social praise.

The "fun you" is the you that gets so excited it's almost embarrassing. To reward your dog, be super-playful and happy. If you feel you're overdoing it, you're probably doing it right. Go overboard. You can't overdo excitement when you're training your dog.

# Consequences

Training involves both rewards and consequences. If you want your dog to follow a leash, for example, but it backs up, don't give in and move toward it. Just wait. Pulling on the leash is an uncomfortable experience for your pup. When they come toward you, they'll soon discover that the leash loosens. Problem solved.

Like all training, this is a lot easier to teach dogs while they're young. If your dog pulls backwards away from you and you give in and go to them, you will teach them that pulling is the way to relieve the pressure. By holding steady and waiting until the dog comes to you, you're teaching it what it needs to do to make itself more comfortable.

## Aversives

One important category of consequences is known as "aversives," meaning unpleasant stimuli intended to curb bad behavior. Most aversives are related to a dog's senses of taste, touch, and sound.

- **Taste:** Aversive tastes are used to prevent a dog from chewing or mouthing what it isn't supposed to. Typical aversive tastes include bitter apple spray, pepper, and vinegar.
- **Touch:** Aversive touch is what your dog doesn't like to feel. This may include sticky surfaces, slippery floors, or aluminum foil. These aversives can be used to curb behaviors like jumping up and counter surfing.
- **Sound:** Sounds a dog finds unpleasant or disturbing can also be used as aversives. Examples are shaker cans, air horns, and whistles.

Aversives are controversial. A lot of people don't like using them because they are uncomfortable correcting either dogs or kids.

However, aversives are an essential tool in properly training any dog. If you only reward your dog, you're not communicating what it shouldn't be doing. The more you communicate with your dog, the faster it will fall in line with your expectations. You need to exercise self-restraint in using aversives. But also exercise self-restraint around not using them.

Make sure aversives have an impact outside of your presence, otherwise you will create a false positive or an owner-present solution. Think about a kid who likes to steal cookies when their parents aren't around. If the only deterrent is the stern voice of a parent, they will soon find ways to get around these aversives.

Remember that, like all rewards and consequences, aversives are relative. Some dogs may love things other dogs will hate.

## IF YOU'RE NOT TRAINING YOUR DOG, YOU'RE GETTING TRAINED

Every moment you're together, you and your dog are learning. You're communicating your desires and expectations, while your dog is doing the same. Whenever a conflict arises, one of you will win.

If your dog barks and you go over and give it a treat, you're communicating that it can get you to come over and feed it by barking. What will it do in the future? Whatever behaviors you reinforce, your dog will do more of them. With awareness, you can strengthen the behaviors you really want.

## Training Opposites

Kids are great at learning different languages. But the longer they stick with a single language, the harder they find it to learn another one.

It's the same with dogs—kind of. When training, you don't want to build too much value into one specific behavior. Make sure you reward both a behavior and its opposite: sit and stand, or come and go away.

What happens if you don't do this? Let's say you reward a dog constantly for coming to you and don't work on getting it to settle? You get arousal issues and a dog that's constantly—almost neurotically—following you around in hopes of a reward. The goal we want to achieve is balance by training opposites.

## Quality over Quantity

In training, quality is more valuable than quantity. Of course, fifteen minutes of training is better than none at all. But a good fifteen-minute session is far better than a longer, unfocused one.

## HOW LONG DOES IT TAKE TO FORM A NEW HABIT?

Twenty-one days or three weeks is the generally accepted minimum amount of time it takes to establish a new habit. According to some studies, the period is as long as two months, but twenty-one days is a good rule of thumb.

If you can get in the habit of creating consistent training schedules for twenty-one days, both you and your dog will be far more likely to meet your goals.

## Lure, Prompt, Verbal Cue

We talked about lure training in Chapter 10. Luring is the first step in a progression that leads up to verbal commands.

Early on, when teaching different behaviors, you're going to lure your dog into position. For example, with "sit," you'll first lure the dog into that position by handling food near the dog's nose and then raising the food over its head. The dog will naturally sit. You're driving the dog.

The first move in the training game is showing your dog that you're offering them something of value. Nonverbally, you're telling your dog,

"Here, come hang out with me. Look what I have for you." If it starts doing what you want, you'll give it something it values. You're exchanging services. The dog's attention is a service to you, and your food is a valuable service to your dog.

Once that's established, you evoke the same behavior with a prompt—a very slight signal or hint that prompts the behavior you formerly lured the dog to do. Now, you turn your wrist over and the dog sits. At that point, you can move from a prompt to a verbal cue—the command "sit."

Once the verbal cue is established, the behavior should become a dance. You don't want to have to say "sit" every time you're going to put a leash on your dog to walk outside. You just walk to the door and the dog sits nicely. Then you put the leash on and say, "Let's go."

You're creating everyday behaviors where you don't have to constantly dictate commands. By doing this, you establish a shared set of experiences. In time, you and your dog can grow to understand each other so well that training becomes like a dance.

## Naming Commands

At first, it's best to be nonverbal when working with your dog. You need to ensure that you can get your dog to produce the exact behavior you're looking for.

When you start using verbal cues or commands, discipline yourself into only giving the command once. People often think repeating a command will let their dog know what they're asking. But if the dog doesn't understand the underlying behavior, it won't know how to respond.

Once it fully understands the behavior, you can associate a word or command with that behavior. At that point, you say "sit" once only. You don't say "sit, sit, sit!"

Remember, a dog's first language is body language. If your dog isn't listening to you, that's either because it doesn't understand what you're asking, or it's distracted. Repeating a command won't fix either of those problems. If the dog is distracted, you have to get it engaged. If the dog doesn't understand, you have to go back to teaching it.

In other words, training doesn't go in only one direction from lure to prompt to a verbal cue. You'll be going back and forth between them frequently.

## The Three-D Ladder

The three D's of the Three-D Ladder are duration, distance, and distraction. As you continue training, you'll move up this ladder: increasing duration and distance and distraction. As with all training, however, this isn't a linear process.

### Duration

Duration is the length of time your dog can hold a behavior, such as a sit, a down, or a settle. Build duration—moving up the ladder— but do so randomly: shorter, longer, medium, shorter, medium, longer, shorter.

When training your pup, don't become predictable. More random input makes the dog an active participant in the learning process. Dogs are good at reading your body language and pick up patterns very well. The more random you are, the better.

### Distance

In moving up the ladder, you want to build in random distances. When teaching your dog to stay, walk one step away, then half a step away, then three steps, one step, ten steps, two steps.

When working on distance, the first five to ten feet are the most difficult. After that point, you'll be able to build in greater distances much more easily without your dog immediately following you.

## Distraction

Dogs are very situational and don't generalize well. This is especially true when working through distractions.

Sometimes you'll need to scale things back. Say you've established a food or reward system, but your dog is distracted by motion at the window and ignores the treat you're offering. You may need to back off of the distraction a bit or start training your dog again during mealtime. The best time to train your dog is when it's highly motivated to take what you're offering.

## Rehearse, Audit, Proof

The three critical steps in moving up the Three-D Ladder are rehearse, audit, and proof. There's forward momentum, but again, the process isn't linear.

- **Rehearse:** Practicing each command, gradually adding duration, distance, and distraction.
- **Audit:** Putting your dog in situations that will test its ability to respond to the command.
- **Proof:** Success at whatever you ask it to do, the first time you ask it.

Just because your dog does something perfectly for two weeks doesn't mean it knows what you're asking it to do. You may soon find yourself saying, "She knows she shouldn't go to the bathroom in the house," or "He knows he should come when I call." Maybe he knows he should come when you call when he's in the backyard, but not when he's playing with his buddy down the street.

In other words, don't feel sure you've arrived at the "proof" stage too early. You're probably still at "audit," the longest stage of the training process. Most of the learning takes place in the audit stage. Proof is the end-of-semester tests. Regularly audit how your dog is doing in different situations, noting what it struggles with and what its strengths and weaknesses are.

Sometimes you'll need to go back to basics. A little refresher course on your expectations never hurts. A behavior is like a muscle. If you don't exercise it regularly, it gets weak.

During the audit phase, keep increasing the three D's: duration, distance, and distraction. Gradually give the dog a bit more freedom. Perhaps take it off leash. Does it come back to you when it's playing with other dogs?

Even during the proof phase, continue to exercise the command and make sure the muscle stays strong.

## Marker Words

In the section on classical conditioning, we discussed "markers." When training, establish a consistent word or sound—like Pavlov's bell—as a marker, to signal that your dog has done a good job. This marker is generally repeated just before giving your dog a treat, so they associate it with the reward. Later, the marker itself becomes a reward.

Good options include "free" and "release." Some people use "bingo." A lot of people use clickers as markers, since the sound a

### CHOOSING A GOOD MARKER WORD

- It should be a word that comes naturally when you're happy.
- It should not be used often in casual conversation.
- It should be short and sharp.
- Only use the word or sound to mark approval when your puppy has done something correctly.
- It should not be confused with your dog's name or actual commands.
- Good marker words include "release," "bingo," or "free."
- Bad marker words include "yes," "good," and "good dog."

clicker makes is very consistent. With our training, this word or sound then becomes a signal for a release.

Don't use a common word as a marker word. Remember, your dog is always listening and responding, like a fluffy satellite dish.

## Stay Away from Stay

Make "stay" part of any behavior you teach. The expectation is that a dog will continue its behavior until it is released. We don't use the word "stay" as a command to make that happen.

When training a behavior such as "sit" or "down," only reward your pup at the moment of release, *not* when they first do what you want. Many people give their pets a reward too early, and the dog understandably assumes the behavior is completed. This training style makes the behavior unstable. As soon as the dog receives a reward, they think, "Great, my work is done. Time to wander off and sniff under the couch."

Let your pup know that sustaining the behavior is what you value, and therefore what gets them access to the goodies.

# CHAPTER 12:

# REMOVING THE STIGMA

You've built a great foundation with your dog. At seven months, it's shown it has the ability to learn, and you have great expectations that it will be the "perfect pet."

Then reality strikes. Suddenly, you find yourself struggling to keep your dog's attention and make sure it's reliably obedient. Like a teenager, it seems more interested in anything that doesn't involve you—its parent.

There's lots of advice out there about what to do when—to mix a metaphor—the chickens come home to roost. Unfortunately, much of that advice consists of blanket statements such as, "You should never use a prong collar." What if you adopt an aggressive dog? What if you're a 120-pound female trying to walk a Rottweiler? Beyond unhelpful dogma—no pun intended—what you really need are reliable results so that both you and your dog can have a better life.

## PROGRESS, NOT PERFECTION

There are perfect pet owners. They just don't have pets yet.

Part of the problem is that humans are selfish. We want to make pets of dogs bred to live in wide open spaces, where they spend their days chasing and herding. We bring them into busy city environments crowded with people and cars, pamper them, and then we wonder why they turn into nervous wrecks.

If you want your dog to be well adjusted, you need to help it exist in the environment where you live.

Let's be clear: A puppy six months or younger is too young to recall or "come" consistently in all circumstances. Implementing a consequence at this stage will do more harm than good. That's why this section is aimed at dogs close to a year and older. Generally, feedback can start at around this stage of a dog's life.

But at this time you can and should have built a relationship with your dog and a strong training foundation, with lots of positive reinforcement. One exception is some aversive consequences for mouthing, biting, and jumping, which you can start a little younger.

If you've adopted an older dog, build a relationship before introducing consequences. This doesn't have to take seven months, but establish trust and expectations before delivering feedback for inappropriate behavior.

## Leveraging Tools

You don't want to rely on your physical strength to work your dog. No doubt you're familiar with the idea that, to a person whose only tool is a hammer, every problem looks like a nail. Build a varied toolbox

### WIN OR LOSE?

Studies on loss aversion have shown that humans are more motivated by the desire not to lose $100 than the desire to win $100. If you're in a weight-loss contest, you're more likely to succeed if you're going to lose $100 if you don't lose the weight, than if you're going to win $100 if you do.

so that you have numerous tools at your disposal, including food rewards, a leash, and tools such as a pinch collar.

Next, learn to use those tools skillfully. An artisan can make much greater use of a set of tools than a guy who's trying to do some DIY for the first time. Use the tools at your disposal to build better communication with your dog and give it clear instructions.

When you're out in public and having a struggle recalling your dog, a food reward is less likely to bring it back than a consequence of some kind. Losing $100 is a better motivator than winning $100.

## Realism Beats Idealism

Some dog training theories insist that all forms of correction are cruel. These ideologies scorn tools such as choke chains and e-collars, insisting on positive reinforcement only. In a perfect world, that sounds great. But we don't live in a perfect world.

Without air resistance, a feather and a rock would fall at the same speed. But air resistance exists. By the same token, distractions exist. Dangers exist. In the world where you and your dog actually live, you may need to use some other tools. That's a controversial position, but it needs to be taken.

We live in the age of the participation trophy. In some schools, every kid involved in an athletic or school activity gets a participation trophy. It's a well-intentioned idea, to reward kids for showing up, no matter how well they do. Unfortunately, it hasn't worked out so well. Many kids who got used to receiving participation trophies while they were at school have had a tough time dealing with real-world consequences as adults.

Not everything comes easy. You have to work for what you want. Learning how to handle stress early in life helps set you up for success later on.

Right now, the dog training world is surfing a similar wave. Yes, there's been some really bad, even abusive dog training in the past. A lot of these new concepts are responses to those problems, which is great. But the pendulum has swung too far in the other direction.

## Create, Connect, Expect

When training your dog, the first step is to create a behavior. Next, connect it, first with a verbal cue or command and, then, with different environments and circumstances. Together, these steps make up the three D's: duration, distance, and distraction.

When the behavior is solid, your expectation is that your dog will exhibit the desired behaviors regardless of what else is happening. What happens when that doesn't happen? You need tools to bring them back into line.

## Fulfilling Your Dog's Potential

Using all your tools—rewards as well as consequences—will help your dog to fulfill its potential. Your task is to enable your dog to succeed in a broad range of circumstances.

That's not going to happen if you only expose it to situations where it's certain to succeed. As the saying goes, "Sometimes you win, and sometimes you learn." That's as true for your pet as it is for business luminaries and sports stars.

Many people avoid putting their dogs in new situations, where they're unsure how the dog's going to respond. Sure, they avoid problems, but they prevent their dogs from working through behavioral issues.

What happens if your dog doesn't come when called? If you rely on rewards, your toolbox is empty. Alternatively, what happens if your dog pulls on its leash when you're out walking and encounter another dog? You could walk the dog at quiet times of day when it's unlikely you'll encounter other dogs, but does this fix the issue?

In the real world, you'll often encounter competing motivators. You may have something appealing to offer, but what does your dog's environment offer? At this point, bribery and rewards aren't enough. You need to find tools able to help steer your dog in the direction you want it to go. And they're out there—if you'll only take advantage and use them.

As the saying goes, "When you're in a hole, the first thing you should do is stop digging." If you're working on a behavior or skill and not getting anywhere, the problem is probably your training method.

## A LITTLE DISCOMFORT
## IS THE PRICE OF SUCCESS

Many people worry that using corrections is cruel. In fact, the opposite is true. What happens when you can't control your dog at the beach or the park? Do you stop bringing it, shrinking its world and limiting its opportunities for play and socialization? Or do you teach it how to behave?

Of course, there's a balance here. Don't swing too far in the other direction and focus only on correction at the expense of rewards. Nonetheless, a bit of discomfort is the price of success. We all know this from our own lives, so why don't we apply it to dog training?

At some point, the value you offer your dog won't be enough to motivate good behavior. If your dog sees a squirrel it wants to chase, no reward you can offer is going to be able to compete as a motivator. Most dogs really like chasing squirrels.

Now, you're feeling conflict and stress. You want your dog to respond differently. What will you do? You need to teach it that unacceptable behavior yields consequences. Training is a constant negotiation, and sometimes you have to be a tough negotiator.

## Responding to Misbehavior

We talked about aversives earlier, but what exactly does a correction involve? Essentially, doing something the dog doesn't like when it misbehaves. This could be making a loud noise, spraying it with a squirt bottle, or tightening its collar. You'll know consequences have been effective if your dog exhibits the behavior less often or stops altogether.

Aim to provide an appropriate consequence, related to the severity of the misbehavior. One good correction is better than ten lousy ones. Some consequences—like saying "no"—are quite gentle. Others are risky because they can make your dog fearful. The only way to avoid complications is to employ them with care.

If your dog is pulling at its leash, and you respond by walking faster, you're building tolerance rather than encouraging good behavior. That's when you can use another tool, like a head halter or pinch collar, that generates enough discomfort to prevent pulling.

If you live near an airport, you eventually tune out the sound of planes. The same principle applies to dogs, except that you don't want them to build tolerance to minor corrections. You need to apply direction to diminish the misbehavior.

A good professional in your local area can coach you on methods and timing. Help is also available through the Mind Your Paws video course, which you can find at mindyourpaws.com.

mindyourpaws.com

## Effective Consequences

Here are some basic guidelines for administering consequences effectively. The stakes are high, and you don't want to get it wrong.

Most importantly, first establish a good relationship with your dog. Positive reinforcement is your primary tool. Establish a level of trust that will compensate for any mistakes if you go slightly overboard on the corrections.

## Timing

Timing is critical. The consequence needs to follow the misbehavior in five seconds or less. Otherwise, your dog will be confused about what behavior is getting corrected.

## TIMING YOUR FEEDBACK

It's a common myth that dogs don't remember. They certainly do. However, what they remember is the association between cause and effect. Remember the ABCs in operant conditioning?

You can't sit down with your dog and explain that, when it chased that squirrel half an hour ago, you weren't mad, just disappointed. You need to apply feedback directly after an undesired behavior, to make sure that your dog is associating it with the correct cause.

## Severity

A consequence should be just severe enough to reduce misbehavior in two to three applications—no more and no less. If the feedback isn't severe enough, it could make your dog less sensitive to future consequences. If it's too harsh, it could physically harm or traumatize your dog. A fearful dog may succumb to additional behavior problems.

## Impersonal

Your dog should not conclude that negative feedback comes directly from you. Otherwise, it may learn to misbehave when no one is looking, or it may decide it doesn't like to be around people. On the other hand, you absolutely do want your dog to associate you with any rewards it gets.

The source of the feedback should be impersonal—like the force of gravity. Many of the most effective tools for doing this act like booby traps.

Although it should go without saying, let's say it: Don't hit your dog. Among other things, that's not the way to give feedback.

## Teach a New Behavior

Undisciplined dogs, like undisciplined kids, can put themselves or others in danger. But yelling at them or hitting them doesn't teach them anything useful. There's a spectrum from highly positive to highly negative, and you don't want to veer toward abuse.

Instead of suppressing behavior you don't like, change it. Don't yell "no" when your dog gets out of control, show or tell it what to do: "Go over there and lie on your bed."

Teach your dog a new behavior to replace a misbehavior. Teach it to "sit" instead of jumping up to get attention. Teach "place" rather than running to the door when the bell rings.

If your dog has no alternate behavior, it may get confused about what it's supposed to do in the situation that caused the misbehavior. It may become stressed and worried or misbehave in some other way.

## Aggressive Behavior

It can be very tricky to apply consequences to aggressive behavior. If your dog has an aggression issue, you're not going to fix it by reading a book. You need to call a trainer.

## Owner-Present Behaviors

Have you ever known a kid who gets scolded a lot by parents? What do they learn? How to avoid scolding, by misbehaving when their parents are out of sight. If you're always applying corrections to your dog, for example, telling it not to jump on the couch, expect it to do just that when you're not around.

To be effective, consequences need to be directly caused by the dog's own behavior. Say your dog jumps on the kitchen counter and a sheet pan falls on top of it, then clatters loudly to the floor. Your dog won't jump on the counter anymore.

## Poorly Applied Consequences

Here are a few examples of what *not* to do when giving your dog negative feedback—and why.

### "Rubbing Your Dog's Nose in It"

This "feedback," which we've discussed before, is generally applied too long after a house-training accident. Your dog won't associate the accident with the consequence. It'll just be confused and scared. Don't humiliate them.

Your dog may learn that it needs to hide from you to poop, which, among other things, will make it harder to potty train your dog.

### Yelling at a Barking Dog

If your dog is barking to get attention, yelling at it may just increase the barking. Mission accomplished! It could also make your dog afraid of you or whomever is yelling, especially if the shouting is accompanied by a physical correction.

This could also convince your dog that what it was barking at was truly important, since its owner is "barking" too. "Great! Let's do this together!"

### Kneeing a Dog That Jumps

Kneeing a dog that jumps up may just teach a dog that people are unpleasant. Or it could reinforce the jumping—if your dog enjoys playing rough, it may learn to jump more aggressively.

## Least Likelihood of Harm

Using consequences properly can be a risky business. When you do, deliver the feedback that has the least likelihood of doing harm.

Relatively harmless consequences include a handclap or a "time out" in the dog's crate. If the dog's misbehavior doesn't lessen after two or three applications, escalation is probably in order.

Many people say, "Don't use a crate as punishment." To an extent, this is true. It's not a good idea to crate your dog in response to specific behaviors. It won't be able to figure out the link between the behavior and the consequence.

On the other hand, there are times when using a crate is appropriate. The first is to keep the dog safe. The second is to give everyone a break. If your dog is running round in circles, the kids are drawing on the wall in crayon, and the dinner is burning, give yourself a break by putting your dog in its crate to decompress.

It's hard to train a dog if you're frustrated, and the crate's a great way to prevent frustration. It's okay to hire a babysitter to watch your child. And it's okay to put your dog in the crate, as a short-term solution that supports long-term training goals.

## Different Personalities, Different Strategies

Every breed of dog has its own drives. Retrievers and herding breeds are highly motivated by social praise. Labs and Golden Retrievers are often called "smart dogs" because of their drive to please. All they want is your love, so when you're disappointed in them, they experience it as a severe consequence.

Other breeds are motivated completely differently. If a German Shepherd or Doberman were affected by a shout or a handclap, it wouldn't make a very good police dog, right? It needs a very different style of feedback. That's also true of hunting breeds.

When administering consequences or corrections of any kind, be aware of your dog's size and personality. A leash correction given to a Yorkie is very different from a leash correction applied to a Rottweiler.

Your dog may seem to be living a happy life restrained by a leash, but it's capable of so much more. If putting an e-collar on your dog allows you to take it off leash and play with it in a park, you're making both your lives better.

Imagine, over time and with the right training, getting your dog to sit on a park bench while you go grab your coffee, and know that it will be lying there waiting for you when you come back. That's a happy, secure dog, and you'll be a happy, secure owner.

# PART VI:

# PAWS TO THE PAVEMENT: TEACHING THE ABCS AND 123S

Well you survived the all-nighters. Barely. Now for the fun stuff. This section covers the training that takes place during this critical time in your dog's development, from about twelve weeks to seven months. You'll learn the foundational, early stages of training that will help you build the best relationship with your dog. If it all seems a bit complicated written down, don't sweat it. All of these commands have a corresponding video, which you can find at mindyourpaws.com.

# CHAPTER 13:

# ATTENTION/FOCUS/ ENGAGEMENT

This step is so crucial I've dedicated an entire chapter to it. I want to highlight not only the value of ensuring you have your pup's attention when training them, but the extent to which many people overlook this phase of training.

Most owners and even some professionals cruise through this step, assuming that the dog in front of them will automatically pay attention. Boy, are they ever mistaken!

Puppies can get distracted by everything from a falling leaf to an unfamiliar noise. And they will. That's why your first priority should be showing your dog that *you* are the value in any environment. Once you have its focus and attention, teaching is a breeze.

Remember, this isn't a linear process. In any phase of training, attention is always your top priority. Sometimes you may need to take a step back to reengage with your pup. Always train the dog in front of you, not the dog you wish you had.

## The Value Proposition

The start of everything you teach your dog is the value in hanging out with you. At first, you want to build that value proposition by giving your dog a reward whenever it comes to you. As we've discussed, the value of the reward depends on the environment you are working in. The more distractions, the more value you will need to offer, especially in the early stages of training. Starting in a relatively neutral environment, such as your living room or kitchen, will yield early success for your dog.

As your dog shows signs of giving you their full attention—shadowing or following you around—you can move to more distracting areas like your backyard, front yard, or local park.

## Loading the Marker Word

Here we will start to cue or initiate the behavior. Don't call the dog's name or say the word "come." Use a random sound like a whistle or a kiss-y noise. You are trying to harness the natural curiosity of your puppy to engage with you when you make any noise.

Typically, the puppy will turn and look or run over to you. When the dog comes to you, you give it the marker word you chose in

Chapter 11. Then you give it its reinforcing reward, which at this point in the training will usually be food.

## INSTAGRAM WORTHY?

Another way of thinking about your marker word is as a snapshot or picture. Over time, you want to create a photo album of acceptable behaviors. The goal is to fill this album with snapshots that capture all three D's—duration, distance, and distraction—so your dog can form an accurate picture of your expectations.

This is how you start turning a secondary motivator into a primary motivator, as discussed in the chapter on learning principles. Your dog's primary motivator is food. You want to link that with a secondary motivator, a marker word like "free!" meaning, "You did an awesome job."

If your dog has difficulty with this process, use a long line—or even a short house line—so they cannot wander too far away.

## Show Me the Money

By loading the marker word or "charging the mark," you're creating an association that, when you say this word, your dog will receive something valuable. This will be the binding contract you have with your dog, and therefore the foundation of your communication.

### Dispersing the Treat

The last thing you want to reward is a dog biting at your hand. If your puppy is nipping or mouthing, be patient and don't release the food until it settles down. If it's very mouthy and bite-y, remove your hand, then put it back and try again.

Make sure your dog gets the food only when it's taking it nicely. This will then become an automatic, default behavior. Your hand position will also help reinforce this expectation. Most people tighten their fists around the food and try to dispense one tiny kibble at a time. Like a Pez dispenser.

Holding your hand like this gives your puppy lots of corners and edges that an excited puppy will mouth and bite at. Instead, put your treats into the palm of a flat, open hand, right at the crease where your palm and fingers meet. Then put your thumb over the food.

Now, your dog's nose can become a food magnet. If you move your thumb slightly, you'll automatically release food that the dog can grab, and it will no longer be constantly chomping at your hand. This also allows you to be in more control of the dog's nose, which you can manipulate through moving your hand. This will be the start of your lure training.

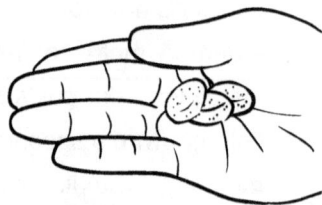

Now both you and your dog are fully prepared for training specific commands—from beginning to advanced.

# CHAPTER 14:

# WHAT EVERY DOG NEEDS TO KNOW

This is where we get real. You've got everything you need to train your pup. This chapter contains everything they need to dog up and become a pleasure to be around. Collectively, the commands in this chapter will take your dog from distraction to focus and self-control, and will help you solve almost any problem you may encounter with your pet.

Just like you, when someone's trying to get your attention while your favorite Netflix show is playing in the background, puppies are easily distracted. Be patient with them while they learn. It's tempting to physically push (mold) your dog into the positions we're about to describe. As much as you can, resist this urge.

You have what your dog wants—food, treats, toys, social praise. You've got the marketing tools. All you need to do is use them to convince your dog to buy into your training. It seems counterintuitive to avoid verbal cues at first, but that's what we'll do. The idea is to build the behavior, then associate the verbal cue. As your prompt or lure becomes less and less important, fade the lure and use the verbal cue, *prior* to the prompt or helper.

Finally, mix it up to surprise your pup. A lot of owners create a standard training routine. When they do this, the dog learns the pattern, rather than distinguishing between unique commands.

## Mark-Move-Merit

This simple concept is the secret sauce. Mama's recipe for perfect dog training, every time. Unlike the typical Italian mama, however, I'm going to spill the cannelloni. Mark-move-merit is the backbone of your training. It's essential that you understand this concept before training specific commands.

When teaching your dog to sit, don't give them a reward when they do what you want. First, **mark** the behavior, letting them know that they have done it correctly. Then, release them and allow them to **move.** They should come to you to receive their reward. Only *then*, when they have completed the command, should you give them their **merit** (a reward). This process creates far more stable behaviors than simply rewarding your dog when they perform a requested behavior.

Now, on to the skills themselves.

# Recall

## Verbal Cues

Come, Here

## Practical Application

The ability to recall, or get your dog to come when you call them the first time, every time, is the most important skill you can teach your dog. "Sixty percent of the time, it works every time" may have been enough for Paul Rudd's Brian Fantana in *Anchorman*, but it won't cut it when you're training your pup.

Once you've trained your dog to recall, you can give it much more freedom. You'll be able to join one another in many more enjoyable activities, trusting that you can get your dog back to you whenever you want.

## Lure/Prompt

If you've been working on the engagement and focus drills we went over in the last chapter, you're most of the way there.

You're getting your dog to come to you because you make a certain sound. The actual sound you make is irrelevant, because you're going to remove it later. What you're doing is getting your dog's attention without calling its name or using a verbal cue like "come" or "here."

When the dog runs over to you, you mark and reward, as described in the last chapter. First you use a marker word like "free" or "release."

Then, one or two seconds later, you give the dog a treat or something else it values.

Initially you may need to mark and reward a halfway point. If the dog takes two or three steps toward you when you make the noise prompt, mark and reward. Then delay the mark and reward until the dog gets closer and closer to you.

## Training Tips

Training is gradual. Start by training the recall with your dog on a long leash in a quiet environment, such as your house. You can then move outside, first to your front or backyard and then to more distracting environments like a park.

If your dog starts struggling, don't pull on its leash. Instead, move away from it, walking backwards. Play hard to get. Once it comes toward you, mark and reward with a treat.

Most people stand when they recall their dog. If you're struggling to get your dog to follow your lead in a standing position, try bending over or kneeling on one or both knees. This turns you into a bigger, low-to-the-ground target for your dog to run to.

Don't show the food reward to your dog to get it to come to you. If you use a treat as a bribe too early in the training process, it will come only when you show it food. When you don't have food, they won't recall reliably. Most of the time, you'll need to recall your dog when it's not looking at you.

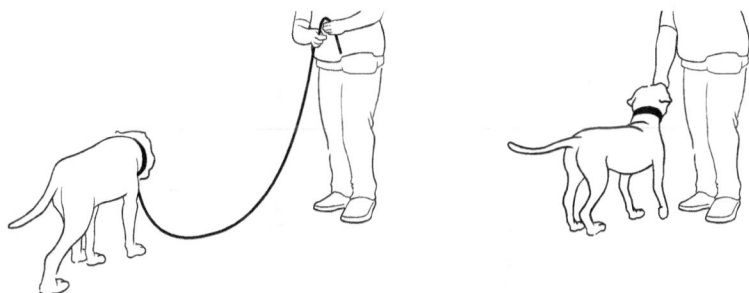

# Spin

## Verbal Cue

On and Off (for Wax On and Wax Off), Left and Right, Spin and Turn, Twist and Shout

## Practical Application

"Spin" teaches dogs coordination. When they can spin, they'll be comfortable using both their front and back legs to move in a tight circle. Your dog will also learn how to turn and face toward you when moving away from you. After a command like "place," you may have a tough time getting the dog to turn and face you after it leaves your side.

## Lure/Prompt

Put a food treat in one of your hands and bend over your dog at a ninety-degree angle. If the food is in your right hand, move your right arm and the treat clockwise. If it's in your left hand, move it counterclockwise.

## Training Tips

- Make sure your dog is in front of you with enough room to turn in a circle, following the motion of the hand with the treat reward.
- Keep the arm circles nice and tight, with your hand and legs close together.
- This is a good command to combine with a "place" and "sit." First, lead your dog onto its bed with a "place." Then get it to spin around to face you. Finally, have it "sit."

# Touch

## Verbal Cue

Touch

## Practical Application

"Touch" is a great way to teach your dog how to use its nose to do things like shut doors or ring a doorbell to go outside to the bathroom.

You can also use "touch" in combination with recall, or "come," to teach your dog to come and touch its nose to you. This is especially helpful for nervous dogs—physical touch is one of their biggest rewards.

## Lure/Prompt

The easiest way to start teaching "touch" is to place a little treat between your middle and index fingers, or between your middle and ring fingers. Hold your hand down near the dog's face until its nose touches you. Then mark and reward.

Next, get rid of the food and put only your hand down for the dog to touch. Mark and reward.

Build up to other objects. If you're going to use an electronic doggy doorbell, hold it down for the dog to see, and then to come and touch. Mark and reward.

Eventually, you'll reach a point where you'll be able to point to something you want the dog to touch. Begin with something they're already familiar with, like the doorbell. Mount the doorbell on a wall and point to it. When the dog touches it, mark and reward.

## Training Tips

- Use different things the dog is used to touching, like a door, as lures.
- Always make sure your dog is comfortable with the object you want it to touch. For example, if your dog is uncomfortable with bells, make sure you get the dog comfortable around those bells before you start teaching it to touch them. You can place the bell on the floor, have the dog eat a meal near the bell, and so on.
- If you're struggling to get your dog to touch an object, put some peanut butter or something else edible on it.

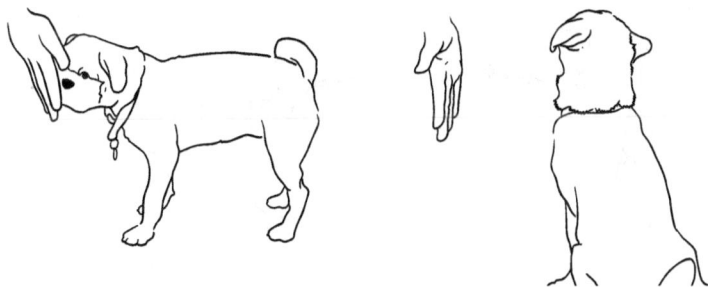

# Weave

## Verbal Cue

Weave, Through, Figure Eight

## Practical Application

"Weave" builds coordination. A lot of dogs, especially small dogs, get nervous around legs and feet. This command gives those dogs confidence, so they're comfortable near your legs and feet.

## Lure/Prompt

Have a food reward in both hands. The hand in front of your legs lures the dog to come to you. Then you bring the hands together under and through your legs. Then continue to lure the dog around one leg by moving the hand in back around it and to the front.

Then repeat the sequence. The hand that was in back is now in front, and vice versa. Lure the dog through your legs and around the other leg. Once you complete one full sequence, mark and reward.

A good way to picture this move is to compare it with dribbling a basketball. You have one hand in front of you and another behind. You start by dribbling the ball with your front hand and then pass it through

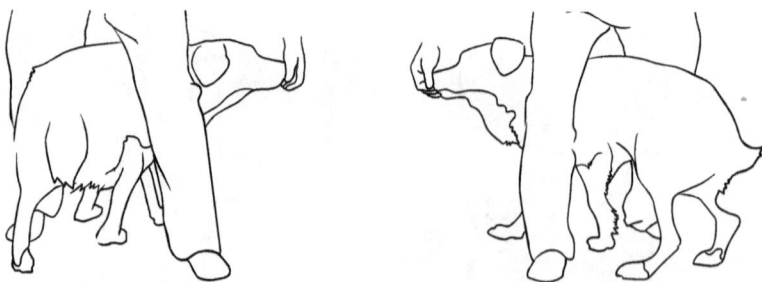

your legs to the back hand. Then you bring the ball around one leg and repeat, with what was the back hand becoming the front hand and the front hand moving to the back. Then repeat, going around the other leg. Finally, apply for you and your perfect pet to join the Harlem Globetrotters as part of the halftime show.

## Training Tips

- If your dog finds it hard to complete both sequences, going around both legs, start by rewarding it when it finishes the first sequence. Then, build up to having it nail the second sequence before receiving a reward.
- Slow down. You're not really dribbling a basketball, and most people bring their hand around too quickly. Go at the dog's speed. Otherwise, it's just going to sit there, watch your hand come around, and think, "Okay. I'll grab the treat when it comes back around to the front."
- Move and shake the hand you want your dog to follow to get its attention.
- Be sure you have food treats in both hands, because you want the dog to follow alternate hands.

# Teardrop (Sitting on Both Sides of You)

## Verbal Cue
Heel, Switch, Left, Right

## Practical Application
When a dog performs a normal "sit," it is directly in front of you, looking at you. But you also want your dog to have the ability to transition to sitting by your side, while continuing to look at you.

## Lure/Prompt
Start with your dog sitting or standing in front of you. Then, put a food reward in one of your hands and move it toward that side of your body, having it pass your legs. When the dog's hind quarters passes your legs, mark and reward. Then, do this with the other hand on the other side.

The next step is to move the hand with the treat out from and then in toward that side of your body in a circular motion. This gets your dog out past your legs and then spins its head toward that side of your body. The goal is to finish with it sitting at your side facing forward.

This is the same sort of circular spinning motion you taught your dog to do in front of you in the "spin" command, only now you're doing it at your side. Your right hand should spin clockwise and your left hand counterclockwise.

Another way to think of this instruction is as a swimming breaststroke. Your arm goes out and your dog goes around you and sits

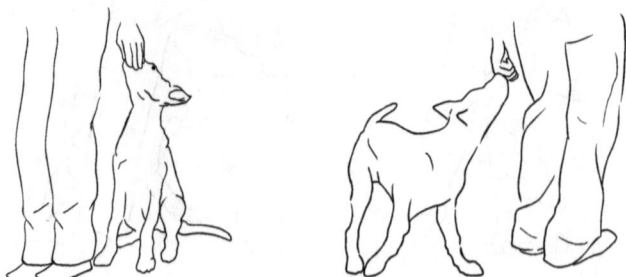

on your left side. With food in your left hand, you lure the dog, then pull the "parking brake" so they stop. There are three steps:

- Have the dog move so its back legs pass to the outside of your legs on the side you want it to go. Mark and reward.
- Spin your dog toward you on one side or the other by moving that hand in a swimming motion—clockwise to the right and counterclockwise to the left. Mark and reward.
- Now, pull your hand back like a parking brake to get your dog to sit by your side. Mark and reward.

As you and your dog gain in confidence, progress so that you mark and reward the last step only. Always work both sides.

## Training Tips

- If you're having a hard time getting the dog to pass your leg line, take a step back with that leg. If you're using your left hand, for instance, step back with your left foot. This will have the effect of making the arm you're signaling with appear longer. Once your dog is on that side, step the leg forward again to meet the other leg, and spin your dog around into a sit.
- You may find that your dog has a tendency to sit next to you with its head facing forward at a ninety-degree angle rather than looking toward you. To prevent this, train using a wall, putting a small distance between the wall and the side of your body you want your dog to sit on. The dog will be more likely to pass your legs and spin around to sit next to you, rather than flaring its body outward.

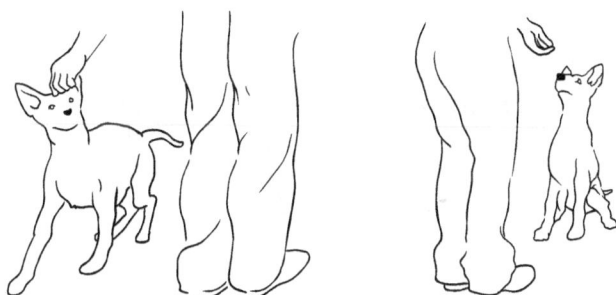

# Between

## Verbal Cue

Between

## Practical Application

Having the control to perform the "between" command with your dog off leash makes it easier to get through busy crowds and other tight places.

You can also teach your dog to put its paws on your feet when in "between," and call that "dance." Unless you want your dog to become a canine Frank Sinatra, however, you may not want to try this at home.

## Lure/Prompt

When teaching this, it's helpful to start with your dog in front of and facing you. Using food as a lure, then "weave" it between your legs and behind you, before getting it to change direction and come back up

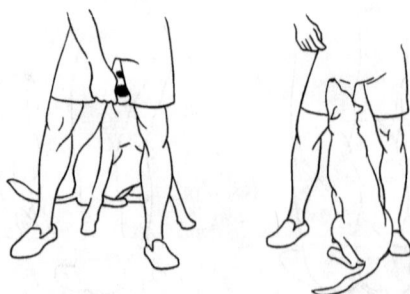

the middle, staying between your legs. Its front legs should line up with yours, as with a good "heel."

Start by taking one or two steps, with the dog staying with you. Mark and reward. Then take a few more steps forward. Mark and reward. You can also get the dog to look up at you while "between." Mark and reward that.

Eventually, increase the number of steps you take before marking and rewarding. You can also start walking backward, making the dog go backward with you, move sideways, and finally turn with the dog.

## Training Tips
- As with "heel," use engagement exercises. You really want to make sure your dog is engaged with you before doing this training.
- If you're struggling with the dog trying to rush out from between your legs, use a leash.

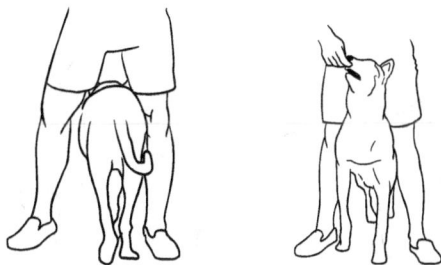

# Sit

## Verbal Cue

Sit

## Practical Application

Sit has a lot of great benefits. Use it to generate everyday obedience, including waiting for food and door manners. By teaching your pup self-control with this command, it'll soon learn that "sit" equals good things.

Ask your dog to sit as a precursor to everything it wants. Have your dog sit for treats and before you walk out the door—in fact, for anything of value. You're showing it how to work impulse control to get what it wants. Does it want to play with a favorite toy? Go see a friend? Borrow the car? The same applies. Okay, maybe not borrow the car. That's a fairly advanced skill.

## Lure/Prompt

Once your dog's engaged with you, think of its nose as a magnet. You're now going to use your hand as the other magnet.

Move your hand down and let the dog's nose connect. Then move your hand up and over its head. Whatever a dog's head does, its rear

will do the opposite. You're getting the dog to look up, and as it does, its butt will go down into a sit.

Stand tall, then mark, take a step away from the dog, and reward it when it comes to you. You're reinforcing the mark-move-merit structure described at the beginning of the chapter.

Don't reward your dog as it sits. Reward it when you release it from sitting, after you give it a marker word like "free."

## Training Tips

- Don't step toward your dog to get it to sit.
- It helps to have your dog's nose aligned in a straight line with its tail before teaching it to sit. If your dog is wiggly and its neck is out of whack, "sit" training is going to be more difficult.
- If your dog is super-excited and starts jumping, don't move your hand. Keep your hand still above its head until it sits nicely. Then mark and reward.
- Randomize the length of time before marking and rewarding.
- You want the dog to sit patiently:
- Randomize the amount of time your dog sits.
- Work your dog through as many variables as you can, adding duration, distance, and distraction.

# Down

## Verbal Cue

Down, Lay, Lay Down

## Practical Application

When you say "down," you want your dog to lie in a relaxed, comfortable position for a prolonged period. Use this command any time you want to leave a dog in a settled position.

## Lure/Prompt

From a standing position, have the dog come and put his nose to your hand with the food facing the dog, like a magnet. You'll then push your hand in and down, almost in a downward slope.

You're moving your dog's head down and almost getting it to bow. The dog's head will now look like an economic downturn—an upside-down V.

Once the dog is in that position, flip your hand. The dog is now looking at the back of your hand. You are communicating that they should not continue to follow the food lure. Try to move your hand slightly away.

Then mark, move a step or two away, and reward. That's stage one.

The process is similar when the dog starts from a sitting position. Put a hand on the dog's nose and push in a downward slope so the dog

## "OFF" OR "DOWN"?

A lot of people use "down" as an aversive or consequence word. If a dog jumps, they yell "Down!"

"Down" should be used as a command, telling the dog to lie down. You don't want to associate the command "down" with messages like "stop doing that" or "bad dog." This just confuses the dog.

"Off" is another word to use when you want your dog to stop doing something. "Off" can easily become a word used specifically to tell a dog to stop what it's doing. What about "no"? "No" is such a frequently used word that your dog is sure to hear it in other, irrelevant contexts, and become confused.

will flop forward. Then flip your hand around, making sure the dog doesn't move. Mark and reward.

In stage two, do the same but put the dog in a full down position before flipping your hand around, then stand up. You may have to move your hand a small distance from the dog before you stand. Then mark, move a step or two away from the dog, and reward.

Your goal is to gradually get to a point where you can stand up fully while your dog stays in its down position. Only then will you mark,

take a step back, and give the dog its food reward. You're teaching the dog how to stay down while you stand up. If you reward the dog when you stand, it will assume that you standing up signals the end of the movement.

## Training Tips

- A lot of people say "sit" to their dogs, and then "down" to make the dog lie down. If you do this, you're merging two commands in the dog's mind. Avoid using them together early on to keep them distinct.
- As with "sit," make sure the dog's body is aligned from nose to tail. "Down" training will be much harder if the dog's body is contorted.
- A lot of dogs don't like to lie down on hard or wet surfaces. Somewhere like a carpet, rug, or its bed is a much better place to teach "down."

# Place/Spot

## Verbal Cue
Spot, Place

## Practical Application

This is a more structured command than "go away." When you give this command, expect your dog to stay in its spot until you release it. The message you're giving is, "Whatever I'm pointing to, get there and stay there."

It helps if you first ask your dog to settle somewhere with a clear boundary or border—a territory it can easily distinguish. In the initial phases, places that are elevated and soft or comfortable work best—a nice, thick, fluffy bed, for example, rather than a hardwood floor or floor mat.

Even in the early stages of training, however, don't limit this command to the same spot. Teach your dog to settle in a number of different places so the command is generalized. You want your dog to understand that "settle" means "chill out wherever I tell you to," not "go to your bed."

As your dog becomes familiar with this command, you can apply it to all sorts of situations, such as when you want them to get into the car, settle down, and stay put for the journey.

## Lure/Prompt

There are five stages to teaching this command.

## Stage One: A Comfortable, Nearby Object

With a food reward in your hand, lure your dog to follow you to, and then onto the object you want it to settle on.

In the early stages, be indulgent, marking and rewarding to get your dog comfortable. At first, the dog may only put its front paws on the object. Mark and reward that. Or it may jump up and then jump off right away. Again, mark and reward. If the object is low to the ground, you might simply lure the dog to walk over it. Mark and reward.

Do this with a number of different objects, such as an elevated bed or an upside-down laundry basket. Let the dog get comfortable with different targets.

## Stage Two: Get On

Once stage one is going well, there's a new goal: get the dog to stop and settle on top of the object. First lure it on top and then into a sit. Mark and reward both stopping and settling.

## Stage Three: Duration

Then, lure your dog on top of the object and into a sit or down. Stand up nice and tall and wait for a random period of time.

Now, get your dog to look at you and mark the behavior with a marker word, like "free." Step back and when your dog comes to you, reward it.

Build up to letting your dog settle for progressively longer periods before marking. As you build to greater durations, be sure to randomize the timing, mixing longer and shorter periods.

### Stage Four: Distance

In this stage, increase the distance between you and your dog. The dog gets up on the object, settles, and looks at you as you start to move backwards, away from it.

The most difficult stage in developing distance will be taking the first three to five steps, so at first take only half a step, one step, or two steps.

When you walk away from the dog, pause. Make sure the dog hasn't moved. Then you'll step back to the dog, mark, step back, and reward when the dog comes to you. Build up two to three steps in this way.

### Stage Five: Distractions

Once duration and distance are going well, start adding distractions to the mix: toys, knocking at the door, ringing the doorbell, dropping food, the ice machine—you get the idea. Slowly build up these distractions over time.

If you can't get the dog to stay in its spot while the distraction is taking place, then a dog who jumps up at the ringing of the doorbell certainly won't settle after you open the door and there's a strange new person in the house, carrying lots of exciting smells.

## Training Tips

- As you get further into training, and your dog has generalized this command, start adding the names of the places where you want your dog to go—for instance, "bed spot" or "crate spot." Put the place name first, not last—"bed spot," not "spot bed."
- At first, keep a leash on the dog so you can guide it in the right direction.
- First make sure each individual stage is going well. Then you can combine stages, picking and choosing when to work on duration, distance, and distraction.

## ALWAYS RETURN

When you're training your dog to "place," always return to your dog to mark and reward. It's essential that your dog understands it's being rewarded to stay.

What happens if you release your dog at a distance and wait for it to come to you before giving it a reward? You're not rewarding it for staying, you're rewarding it for coming. Imagine the doorbell rings and you want your dog to stay in its bed. Teach it to wait there until you come back to it with a reward.

- To repeat, because it's so crucial: always mark and reward only after you return to the dog. Having the dog come to you is completely counterproductive.
- You can also use down instead of sit, or if the dog lies down after a period of time this is okay.

# Stand

## Verbal Cue

Up, Stand

## Practical Application

Wiping paws, bathing, or grooming? The "stand" command will make them all much easier! Just tell your dog to "stand" when you want to groom it, brush it, examine its paws, or give it flea medicine.

"Stand" will make your dog much easier to live with. Now you won't have to fight with it while doing a little grooming. It helps dogs understand better how their hind legs work. It's one of the most underutilized commands but can and should be used every day. Every groomer in America wishes every dog they worked with knew how to stand!

## Lure/Prompt

From a "sit" or a "down," it's easy to teach "stand" using the magnet technique described earlier. Your dog's nose is one magnet and your hand is the other. First, your hand, which is flat with fingers pointed to

the ground, goes to the dog's nose. Then you move your hand upward and toward you to bring it up into a stand.

Don't move your hand too far toward you, as this will make your dog want to step into you rather than simply stand. You want the dog to stand, not walk forward. Once the dog stands, mark and reward the behavior.

## Training Tips

- To keep your dog from stepping forward while doing a "stand," play around with the level of your hands. Sometimes your hands should be a little higher, so the dog looks up. Sometimes you'll want the dog to look straight at you.
- If you want to bring your dog from a sit into a stand, it can help if you get the dog to look down first. Do this by moving the lure toward its chest. The dog looking down helps make its butt go up. Again, the butt and the head go in opposite directions.
- As with other commands, you want to build duration. Randomize timing, varying back and forth between shorter and longer "stands," before you mark and reward.

# Leave It

## Verbal Cue
Leave It, Off

## Practical Application
Everyone knows that toast always lands butter side down. What's not so well known is that there's usually a dog waiting to hoover up the delicious mess as an impromptu snack.

Use this command when you want your dog to leave something alone. Aside from teaching the dog manners, this often has safety implications. Substitute the toast for a bar of chocolate—delicious but toxic to dogs—or a sharp chicken bone, and you'll get the idea.

## Lure/Prompt
Drop a piece of food on the floor. When your dog goes for it, cover it with your hand. As soon as the dog exercises impulse control and stops trying to reach the food, mark and reward.

But don't reward your dog by giving it whatever's on the floor. That would be counterproductive. Give it a different treat with your other hand, preferably one more valuable than what's on the floor.

In stage two, start removing your hand from the treat on the floor, asking your dog to ignore the food even though it's accessible. But be ready to cover it again when necessary. Keep working until your dog shows no more interest in the treat. Then mark and reward it with a treat of greater value.

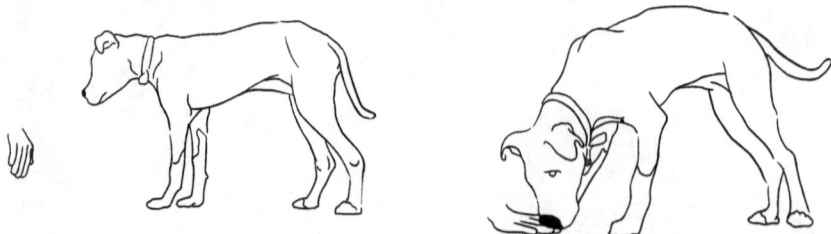

## EXTREME FOOD DRIVE

"Leave it" is a relatively challenging command, so for most dogs you may want to wait a little before teaching it. There's an exception to every rule, however. In this case, you shouldn't wait to teach "leave it" to a dog with an extremely high food drive. If you need to bring your pet's food drive down, teach "leave it" early.

In stage three, once your dog consistently leaves the treat that's on the floor, you can start giving it first a marker word—like "free"—and then a secondary release command—like "take it" or "go ahead"—that allows it to take the treat it had earlier left alone.

## Training Tips

- A lot of people teach "leave it" right away. But there is a risk of damaging motivation, especially when a dog has a low food drive. Hold off teaching "leave it" until you're sure your dog's motivation to learn is strong.
- You can combine "leave it" with "sit" or "down."
- Using "take it" or "go ahead" after "leave it" is a good way to reward distance. You drop a treat on the floor and the dog "leaves it." Then move farther away, mark, and finally reward by allowing the dog to grab the treat in front of it.

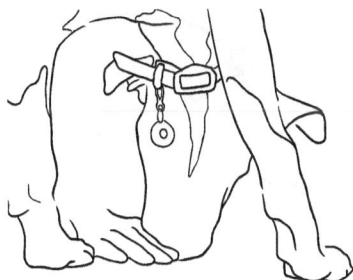

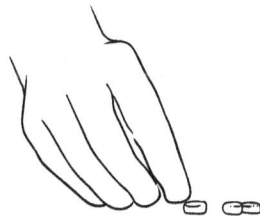

# Loose Leash Walking

## Verbal Cue

Heel, With Me, Let's Go

## Practical Application

Loose leash walking is your most valuable training tool. In loose leash walking, your dog's front legs line up with your legs. It's not pulling at the leash but staying beside you in a loose, relaxed walk.

You want your dog to be an active participant in your walk and stay off Nosebook—the distracted sniffing around characteristic of canine social media. You don't want a dog that keeps pulling at the leash on walks or cuts you off and trips you up. When your dog is following your stride pattern, it's also easy to keep an eye on them.

Aligning your dog's front legs with your legs gives it mental stimulation on the walk. Its job becomes staying with you on the walk, making it an active participant, not a passive recipient.

Walks should be both a bonding experience and a time for training. Every time you step out the door together, you're training your dog to move through a variety of environments without pulling or getting distracted. No matter how busy you are, you need to walk your dog, so take advantage of walks—as you do with mealtimes—for training. Don't waste time when walking!

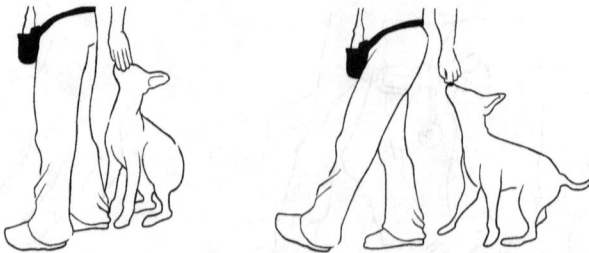

## Lure/Prompt

This is like putting the carrot in front of the proverbial donkey. Take a treat in your hand and hold it by your side—slightly in front of you, signifying where you want the dog to walk. You can also tap the side of your leg.

At the end of the "heel," have your dog sit. Then mark and reward. At first, the "sit" should follow soon after you start walking. Gradually lengthen the time between starting the "heel" and stopping, having the dog "sit," and marking and rewarding.

## Training Tips

- As a first step, use engagement exercises to make sure your dog is involved with you and not with the surrounding environment. Make a noise of some sort to have the dog come over to you, and then mark and reward. What you're doing is making yourself more valuable than the environment.

- In the beginning, don't worry about walking a long distance. Build up over time. Quality over quantity. You may start out by walking back and forth in front of only one house for a pre-specified length of time. Then move up to two and then three houses. And so on.

- Don't start out doing a great loose leash walk, and then get tired and let your dog pull you all over the neighborhood. This just creates bad habits. As always, be consistent and patient. Do as much as you can, but no more.

- Once you've established a good pace, speed up and slow down slightly to check whether the dog is still engaged.
- When you stop, your dog should stop right next to you. If you're walking fast, slow down before you stop. You want to make sure your dog is able to stop when you do.
- Have your dog maintain a nice "heel" until you finish with a "sit," then mark and reward. Now, the dog can do whatever it wants to do—sniff, smell, go to the bathroom, or greet another dog. But not before.

# CHAPTER 15:

# PARLOR TRICKS WITH A PURPOSE

You don't take your four-year-old to soccer training with the expectation that they'll become the next Lionel Messi or Cristiano Ronaldo. You do it because playing soccer is a way for them to have fun, socialize, and develop motor skills, self-confidence, and self-esteem.

The same principle applies with the commands in this chapter. Sure, they look cool. But you're not teaching them because you expect your dog to win a "best in show" rosette. The benefits are far more immediate than that. For example:

- **Offset boredom.** Both dogs and people eventually get bored working on the basic commands covered in the last chapter. Give your dog a new challenge and it'll be fun for you both.
- **Increase social interaction.** Who doesn't like to show off parlor tricks—or watch them? Giving your dog a party trick increases motivation and boosts active participation in training.
- **Increase concentration, focus, and mental capacity.** These tricks push both dogs and their owners. Your dog will break through earlier learning limitations and become (even) smarter.
- **Competition.** Competing for rewards bolsters drive for both treats and overall performance.

* **Work ethic and responsibility**. These commands help dogs control their arousal level, making them less distracted and entitled and more responsible.

Last and certainly not least—these commands are fun, for both you and your dog!

# Play Dead

## Verbal Cue
Play Dead, Bang!

## Practical Application
"Play dead" is another way to get your dog to settle. You can't have too many of these tools in your repertoire! It's also useful when your dog needs to be inspected, for example, when it's at the vet or the groomer. Finally, it's a critical prerequisite for the ever-popular "roll over" command.

## Lure/Prompt
First, put your dog in the "down" position. Then, curl the hand holding the treat under its chin, toward the side it will end up lying on. Mark and reward.

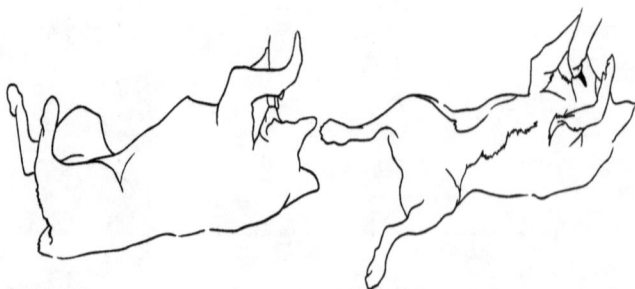

When a dog makes this movement, most will settle to one side or another—not both. After you put your dog in a "down," notice which side their hips are going to settle and go in that direction.

## Training Tips

- Remember to start with the reward up toward the dog's head, then move it down the chest line. But don't move the reward too far toward your dog's back legs, otherwise it'll respond by contorting into a "C" shape rather than lying flat on its side.
- Don't compete against the way your dog's hips settle naturally. Have it "play dead" on the side its hips naturally fall.

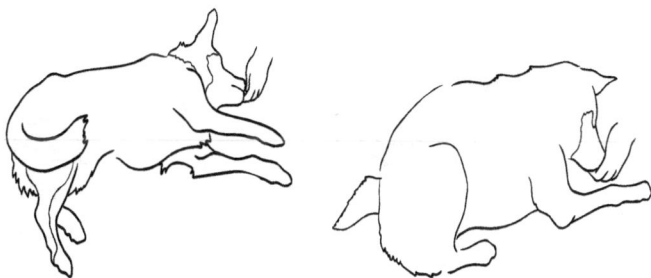

# Roll Over

## Verbal Cue

Roll Over

## Practical Application

"Roll over" teaches your dog important motor skills. It can help nervous dogs feel comfortable with you standing over them when they're lying down. And yes, it's a lot of fun for the whole family and a great way to impress your friends!

## Lure/Prompt

"Roll over" is a continuation of "play dead." First, put your dog in the "down" position. Then curl the hand holding the treat under its chin toward the side it "plays dead" on.

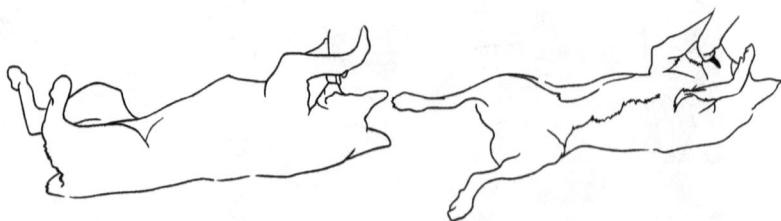

Once your dog's on its side, continue to move the lure down the dog's chest line. When the dog commits to rolling on its back and onto its other side, take a side step. Then mark and reward.

## Training Tips

It's important to move the lure down the dog's chest line but not too far toward its back legs, which contorts the dog into a "C" shape. Once that happens, it won't be able to roll over because its shoulder will be locked to the ground.

Don't move your hand away too quickly. Remember, "roll over" is step three in a three-step process: "down," "play dead," and "roll over."

As with "play dead," your dog will have a natural tendency to lie on one side or another. Go with that rather than resisting it. If you want, you can eventually teach your dog to roll over in both directions, but that's more advanced training.

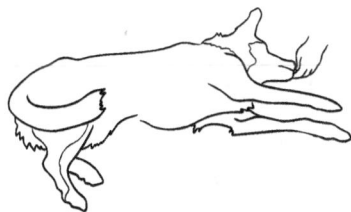

# Shake

## Verbal Cue

Shake, High-Five, Paw, Bump

## Practical Application

Like so many of these commands, this is fun. It helps your dog separate its left front from its right front paw. It also prepares your dog for other tasks it can do with one of its paws, like closing a door or ringing a bell.

## Lure/Prompt

You're training the dog to shake with both its front paws. Unlike "play dead" and "roll over," you do want to be able to switch sides with "shake."

There are two ways to teach this skill. In both, start with the dog in a "sit," with its weight distributed equally between its front paws.

In the first variation, hide a piece of food underneath your right hand and place it on the ground near the dog's left paw. When the dog paws at your hand, mark and reward.

Then gradually work on lifting your hand, until the pawing becomes a "shake." Do this on both sides. This is the more popular way to teach "shake."

The second variation again starts with your dog in a "sit." This time hold the food lure in your hand, to the dog's nose. If it's in your

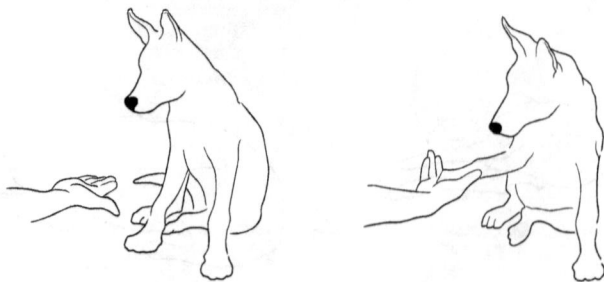

right hand, move it slightly to the left. If it's in your left hand, move it slightly to the right.

This will change the balance of the dog's front paws. If you move slightly to your right, with the treat in your left hand, the dog will put its weight on its left paw and its right paw will come up. Same for the other side.

At first, don't try to grab your dog's paw. When one of its paws comes up naturally, mark and reward. Once this is established, put your left hand out to the right side or right hand out to the left. By doing this, you're indicating the paws you want lifted and put in your hand to "shake." When this happens, mark and reward.

Training Tips

In both versions of this command, keep your hand steady while it's above the ground. Don't move it down toward the ground or toward your body, even when you're bending down. If your hand goes down, the dog will go into the "down" position. If your hand moves toward your body, the dog will be forced into a "stand."

A lot of times it can help if you push slightly into the dog and then move your hand over. Pushing your left hand slightly into the dog and to the right will get the dog to lift its right paw up.

Don't lift the dog's paw or leg yourself. If it needs a little help sometimes, you can tap the lower joint where the paw meets the leg with your index or middle finger. That's a helpful cue that says, "Hey, I'm looking for you to lift your hand here," without you having to grab the dog's paw.

# Crawl

## Verbal Cue

Crawl, Get Low

## Practical Application

Having your dog stay in a low position while moving forward is a great coordination skill.

## Lure/Prompt

Put your dog in the "down" position. Then move the hand with the food reward away from its nose to keep it down while moving forward. Mark and reward.

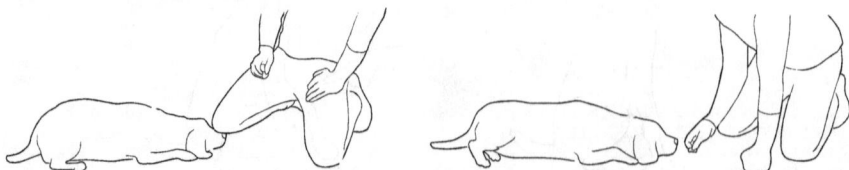

## Training Tips

- Put the hand without the food reward toward the dog's hind legs, almost like a wall or ceiling, so it can't get up. Float that hand above the hips so that, if the dog tries to stand up, it feels the hand and moves back into a "down."

- You can also teach this by putting a chair over your dog, so it naturally crawls forward between the legs of the chair without standing up. You can then put two and then three chairs together and teach the dog to crawl underneath the tunnel. Eventually, you can remove the chairs so the dog crawls on its own.

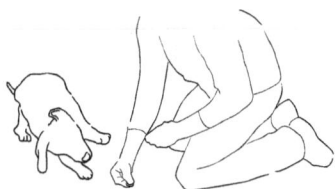

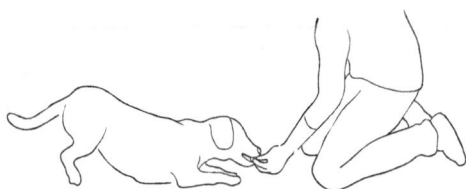

# CHAPTER 16:
# PUTTING PUPPY POWER INTO PRACTICE

Training your dog isn't just for show. It also makes your life easier. This is where the rubber really meets the road. Or, as the title of this part of the book suggests, the paws meet the pavement. In this chapter, we'll apply the commands and skills we covered in the previous two chapters to a number of real-world scenarios. These are things you do with your dog on a regular basis, whether every day or annually.

These are more advanced behaviors that depend on previous training. However, don't wait too long to start teaching them. It's important to work them into a regular training regimen, not limit them to special occasions.

Use training times to accustom your dog to different tools and environments. Then, when you perform a task, you've already worked through most of the issues, including touching and positioning your dog in specific ways. Everything depends on building a trusting relationship with your dog. That's both the foundation and purpose of all training.

Owners get in trouble by trying to get their dog into a crate only when they're leaving the house. First get your dog comfortable in a crate while you're around! If you're going to bathe your dog in a tub, make sure it's familiar with how it feels to get and be in the tub before giving it a bath.

# Holding the Dog's Collar

## Prerequisites

"Sit," "down," or "place," depending on the situation and your dog's energy level

## Practical Application

Collars are safety mechanisms. It's useful to teach your dog how to settle while you touch its neck to attach or remove a collar, or even grab that collar if necessary, for example, if it starts running into the street. You want your dog to be comfortable with restraint. While this may seem basic, the last thing you want to do is restrain your dog without using appropriate commands. If you do that, you'll end up fighting your dog, which is in no one's best interests.

## Lure/Prompt

Start with the collar on the dog's neck. Then start petting around its neck. When your dog remains calm and settled while you do this, mark and reward.

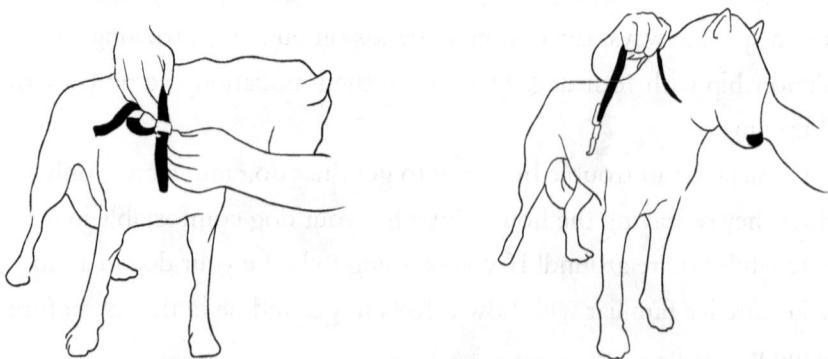

Once that is established, start holding the collar. Mark and reward. Then mark and reward when you release the collar.

You're getting the dog comfortable with you grabbing its collar, letting go, and then grabbing and letting it go again. Also work on taking the collar off and putting it on again several times. Mark and reward only if the dog is settled.

## Training Tips

- Do this when your dog is in a "sit," a "down," or a "place" or "spot."
- If your dog is more relaxed, "sit" or "down" will work.
- Many dogs find physical touch a big reward. During training, these dogs could go a bit crazy and start jumping on you.
- You can also start introducing "place" on a raised platform while holding the collar, so it can't jump around without falling off.

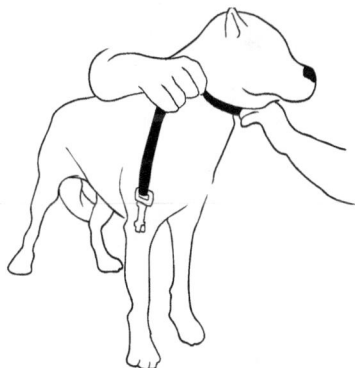

# Putting on a Leash

## Prerequisites

"Sit," "place," or "spot," depending on your dog's activity level

## Practical Application

There's no substitute for good manners. You shouldn't need to struggle when putting your dog's leash on.

## Lure/Prompt

This isn't easy. You want your dog to happily sit while you attach a leash, not grudgingly comply or—worse—struggle with you. Don't rush through an earlier step to get to the next one. If you put your dog in a "sit" and it gets up when you pick up its leash, work on the "sit" again, making sure you can present the leash without the dog moving.

Reach a point where your dog can remain calm while you pick up the leash, touch or hold its collar. If the dog moves, work through the "holding the collar" steps again. Then you can work on snapping on the leash.

Don't let your dog get up before you mark. Expect it to stay sitting until you give it a marker like "free!" The dog can then move and get its reward—going outside.

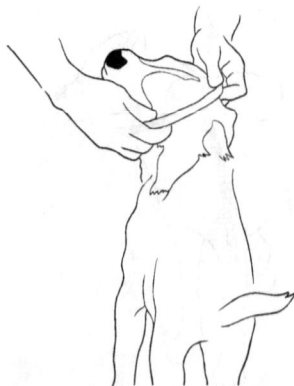

# GREAT, THE OUTDOORS!

Going outside is one of your dog's biggest rewards. Don't waste it. Like mealtimes or walks, putting your dog's leash on is one of the best times for training. They know they're about to go out and play and they're excited, so you can use the experience as a teachable moment.

Make your dog work on arousal control *before* going outside, and the lesson will stick. If you let your dog move around while you're trying to attach its leash, you're losing an excellent opportunity to strengthen good behavior.

## Training Tips

- Putting the leash on is not a cue for the dog to get up from a sit. Your dog should wait patiently while you pick up your keys, grab poop bags, and shovel a handful of treats into your pocket. Your aim is to create a strong command that resists distractions.
- It can't be said too often: Going outside is one of your dog's biggest rewards. Make it pay off.

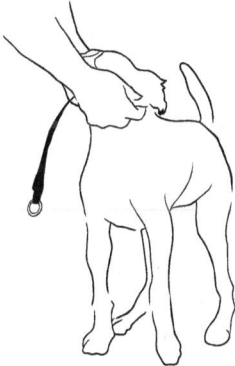

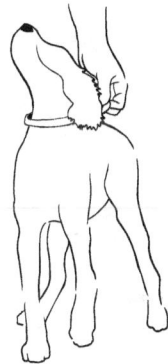

# Leash Pressure Introduction

## Verbal Cue
None

## Practical Application
To get your puppy comfortable wearing a collar and a leash. You want them to learn how to turn off leash pressure. When they feel pressure on the leash, they should follow, as though the leash were a steering wheel. When this skill is ingrained, you can easily guide your dog's movement.

## Lure/Prompt
Start by putting the leash in the same room as your dog, letting them sniff it and get used to it. Then, attach the leash and let your dog drag it around without you holding it. You want the dog to wear the leash and drag it around until it gets comfortable wearing it.

Next, take hold of the leash and add a little tension to drive your dog into different positions. The purpose of this stage is to get your dog used to feeling tension on the leash. This creates a boundary. At first, your dog will probably struggle against this inhibition of its behavior.

When your dog starts struggling with the leash, add a little more pressure. Don't pull. Simply stand there, wait, and allow the dog to continue to resist the leash tension. I know it's tempting but don't give in. Continue holding pressure to the leash. Then, when the dog comes over to you, mark and reward.

Now, start moving the leash around. For example, if the dog is sitting in front of you, you might take the leash and move it with your right hand to make the dog come to your right-hand side. Mark and reward.

Then, put the leash in your left hand, creating tension so that the dog has to come to your left side. Again, mark and reward.

## Training Tips

- When you're starting Leash Training 101, use a house leash—a shorter leash without a loop for you to hold on to. You'll hold the straight end of the leash instead.
- Your aim is simply to get the dog comfortable wearing a leash and responding to pressure. You're not trying to break any land speed records the first few times you take your pup out for a stroll. Far better to relax and enjoy the sights (while they enjoy the smells).
- Don't fall into a predictable pattern. Your goal is to get your dog to respond to the command you give it, not for it to fall into a routine of anticipation.

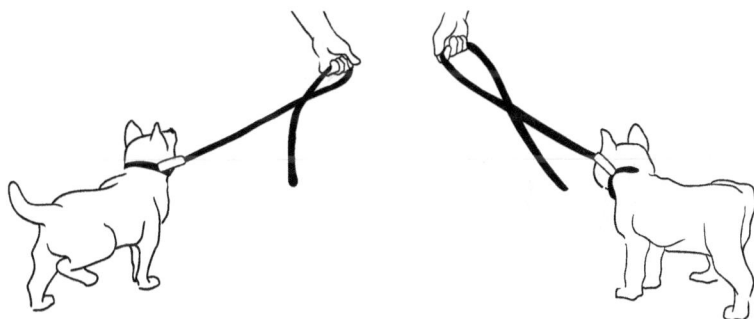

# Getting in the Tub and Standing for a Bath

## Prerequisites

You'll need to teach your dog "place" or "spot" before moving on to this command. You'll also use "sit."

## Practical Application

Dogs get dirty!

## Lure/Prompt

They say there's more than one way to skin a cat (no cats were skinned in the writing of this book). There's definitely more than one way to give your dog a bath. The right option for you probably depends on the size of your pup.

You may choose to bathe your dog in the tub or a walk-in shower, or you may prefer to shower it outside, using a hose. If you're doing the latter, it's a good idea to have it "spot" onto a platform, for example, a small recycling bin or a large storage container that's been flipped upside down.

Wherever you bathe your dog, the basic principles remain the same. To begin with, use a leash. It's hard to catch and manipulate a wet dog without one!

The process is gradual. The first step is to get your dog to settle wherever you want to bathe it, whether in a tub or outside. Use the

leash or treat to guide your dog into the tub or onto your designated platform. Put the dog in a sit. Then mark and reward. At this point, all you're doing is helping your dog feel comfortable getting in and out of the tub or on top of the platform.

The next step is introducing your dog to the hose, spray, or tap— whatever you'll use to bathe it. At this point, don't spray the dog with water, unless you enjoy chasing a wet dog around your home or garden! Restrict yourself to turning the water on and off while the dog stays in position. Again, mark and reward.

Then, without turning on the water, put the dog in a "stand" and start lifting its paws. Alternate between a "stand" and a "sit." Mark and reward.

Once all of the above is going well, you can start introducing some gentle water spraying. Then the shampoo.

## Training Tips

- Use a leash—whatever kind of leash works best for you and your dog. You don't want to manhandle a wet dog, especially if you don't want to get soaked yourself!
- Take it slow. Some steps will be easier than others. Go at whatever pace works for your dog. If your dog likes water, it may be very easy to turn the water on and off, but it may be very hard for it to jump up on the platform. Or vice versa. Every dog will have its own little nemesis. Take your time working through whatever bothers them.

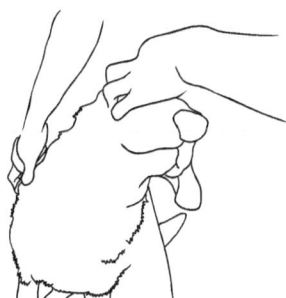

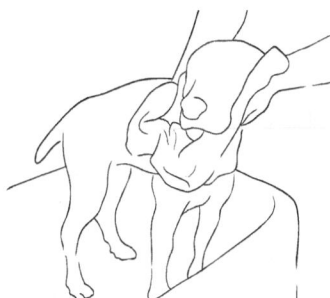

# Presenting Paws for a Nail Trim

## Prerequisites

You need your dog to be comfortable with the "shake" command before you can teach them to sit still while their nails are trimmed.

## Practical Application

You could go to a groomer to get your dog's nails trimmed. But it's a big time and money saver if you can trim them yourself. Also, we've talked about the advantages of being able to take care of your own dog. This will build your relationship with your pet as well as your own confidence.

## Lure/Prompt

Like standing for a bath, the nail-trimming process consists of several steps. After the "shake" command is well established, the next step is to get your dog comfortable with whatever trimming tool you plan to use.

Don't start clipping your dog's nails just yet. All you want to do is introduce it to the tool or tools you're going to use later. You can use one of two different tools: a canine nail clipper or a power tool called a Dremel, after its brand name. The choice is yours.

First, bring the tools out. Then pretend to start work by going through the motions of clipping or turning the Dremel on and off. This will help your dog get comfortable with the sound or the noise of the Dremel power tool.

Once the dog is accustomed to this sound, start by trimming just one nail. Do this on a front paw unless you're a glutton for punishment. Then give the dog a break. Now cut a couple more nails. Work up gradually to all the nails on all four paws. Mark and reward at each stage along the way.

## Training Tips

- Use "spot" or "place" to restrict your dog's movement.
- Use treats as rewards throughout.

# Teeth Cleaning

## Prerequisites

It's important that your dog is comfortable with "stand" and "spot" before you train them to stay still and get their teeth cleaned.

## Practical Application

There's a direct link between a dog's oral health and its life span.

Most pet dogs eat kibble, which doesn't help to keep their teeth clean. In the wild, dogs would eat raw bones that clean and scrub their teeth. Domesticated dogs don't have that advantage.

How many times should you clean your dog's teeth each year? Ask your vet!

## Lure/Prompt

The trick to successfully cleaning your dog's teeth is getting it to keep its mouth open while you're brushing.

It's good to have the dog sit on a crate or other elevated platform. Get the dog nice and high. Then, get the dog comfortable with you petting its muzzle. This shouldn't be hard to do. Once that's going well, start lifting its lips, again in a playful, petting manner. Next, begin rubbing the dog's teeth. When all of the above is progressing smoothly, you can introduce a toothbrush or other cleaning tool.

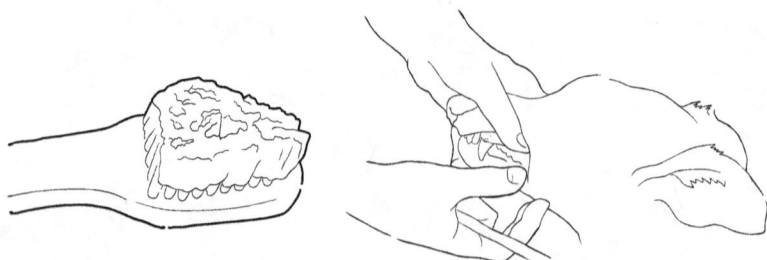

There are a couple different tools you can use. A toothbrush is one option, of course. Another is a finger-cap brush that slips onto the tip of your index finger.

At this point, as with nail clipping, introduce your dog to the toothbrush without actually using it. Allow your dog to take an interest in this new "toy," playing with it while you're holding it. If you're using a finger cap, touch the dog's muzzle and mouth, and then its teeth.

Once your dog's comfortable with all of this, work in some brushing motion. Initially, you're not trying to clean the dog's entire mouth. You're just trying to get it comfortable.

Finally, add some edible canine toothpaste and brush. If you use edible canine toothpaste, you won't need to rinse the dog's mouth after brushing.

## Training Tips

- One reason you're putting the dog on a platform is to restrict its movement. It's helpful to use something elevated so you don't have to bend over when trying to brush its teeth.
- Have food treats ready and reward your dog after each step of this multistep process.

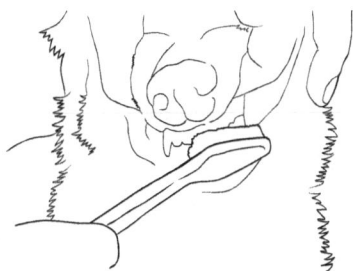

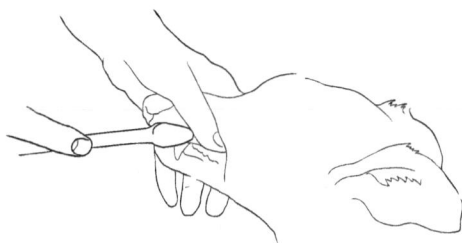

# Swallowing "Naked" Pills Not Wrapped in Food

## Prerequisites

A dog that likes food!

## Practical Application

The easiest way to give your dog pills is to add them to their food. But this doesn't always work.

Some dogs won't eat a pill in their meal. They'll pick it out. And some medications can't be taken with food. But you still need to keep your dog healthy.

## Lure/Prompt

A fun way to begin teaching this skill is by tossing food and having your dog catch it in its mouth. Use a hot dog, cheese, or something similar.

Once that's going well, add an empty gelatin capsule to the food. Before too long, you will be able to toss an empty capsule to your dog and expect them to catch it.

Next, fill the capsule halfway, then completely full, with something that's not a medication. Take the process step-by-step and eventually, the dog will be willing to catch and eat a full medication capsule or pill on its own.

You can also try presenting the gelatin capsule, followed by a treat. For some dogs, this creates urgency to swallow the tablet, so they can get the treat.

## Training Tips

One good sequence is: hot dog or cheese; half hot dog, half-filled capsule; half hot dog, full capsule; capsule only. Experiment, as your mileage may vary.

You can get empty gelatin capsules at almost any pharmacy or health food store.

This works for supplements as well as medications.

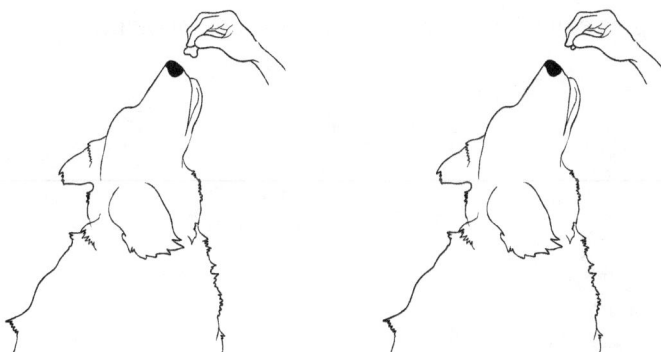

# Tolerating Brushing and De-Matting

## Prerequisites

You can use "spot" or "place" to restrict your dog's movement. This command will keep them in easy range. If having a puppy in the house has already aged you ten years, at least you won't need to strain your aching back further to reach them. Small victories.

## Practical Application

Sometimes your dog's hair is messy and needs brushing. Matting is a condition in which a long-haired dog's hair wraps around itself, and can be quite painful for your pup.

Unless you want your dog to look homeless, proper grooming is important. Removing hair mats also helps your pet to stay pain-free and healthy.

## Lure/Prompt

First, get the dog comfortable in the place and position where it'll be groomed. This is very similar to preparing for bathing. Massage your dog to increase its comfort level.

Once your dog is comfortable and isn't jumping off the spot or running away, bring out the grooming tool or tools you'll use.

We talked about brushes and other grooming tools in Chapter 6. The tools you use will depend on the task at hand. Are you brushing your dog or entering into a major de-matting mission?

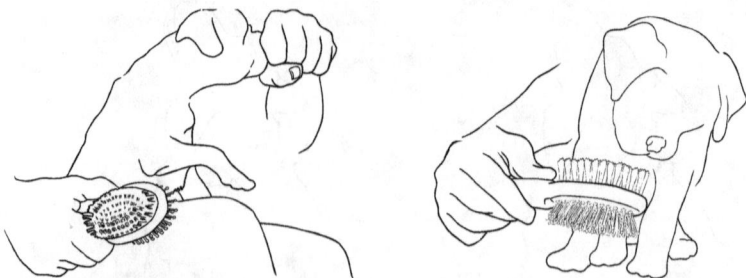

If your dog's fur has mats, you'll need a special comb called a rake. If you're just brushing, you have a ton of options—short bristles, long-wire brushes, and so on. The best choice depends on what kind of dog you have, the length of its hair, and whether the hair is straight or curly.

Bring out whatever tool you'll be using and get your dog comfortable with it. Then, start massaging your dog again, while adding some grooming. Massage and pet your dog, lifting its paws, and making it stand up and sit down, all while you continue to brush and comb it.

## Training Tips

- Get your dog comfortable with light brushing before you start de-matting. De-matting is like untangling your own hair and, as you may know, can be painful.
- Take it slow. All this needs to take place over several days or even weeks. You won't be able to start de-matting after five minutes of light brushing. Stay patient and realize that just because you want things to happen right away doesn't mean they will.
- By this point, you've probably noticed that there's a lot of overlap in the skills in this chapter. You'll use "spot" or "place" when brushing just as you did when bathing or nail clipping. Also use a leash. Once one of these behaviors is established, you'll be able to move right on to the next, building on the foundations you've created.

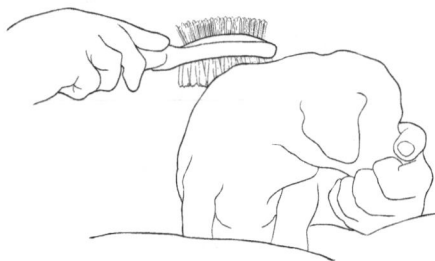

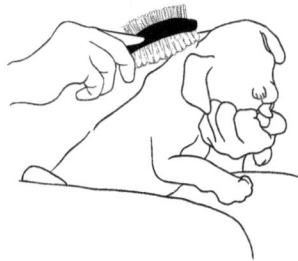

# Lying on the Side While Being Manipulated or Massaged

## Prerequisites

"Play dead"

## Practical Application

A lot of vet visits require your dog to lie on its side as calmly as possible. At home, you'll want your dog to do this in order to inspect it—for ticks, for instance. If your dog has something in its paw or may be injured, you want to be able to check what, if anything, is wrong. There are any number of reasons you may want or need to inspect your dog closely.

## Lure/Prompt

Start by getting your dog to "play dead."

Here's a reminder of how to do this: First, get your dog in the "down" position. Then, curl a hand holding a treat under its chin, toward the side it will end up lying on. Mark and reward.

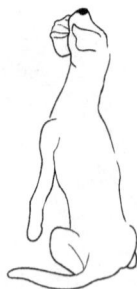

As we discussed in Chapter 14, most dogs will fall and settle to one side. After you put your dog in a "down," notice what side their hips will naturally settle and go in that direction.

Then add on, slowly manipulating your dog. Move its legs around, starting with the back legs. Touch and inspect its belly. Then move on to inspecting the entire dog.

## Training Tips

• Mark and reward as often as necessary as you continue with your inspection.

• If you discover an injury or similar problem, get to the vet.

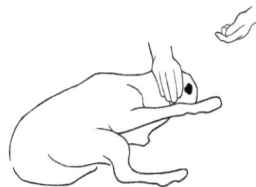

# Staying Still for Injections, Blood Draws, and Thermometers

## Prerequisites
"Touch"

## Practical Application
Going to the vet is stressful. If your dog is moving around nervously, its anxiety festers and grows. If you can help it settle while the vet examines or treats it, the vet won't need to grab or restrain it, making the visit far less of an ordeal.

## Lure/Prompt
Establish a good "touch." Reach a point where your dog is willing and able to touch your hand for an extended period. Build and

randomize duration with the "touch" command. Mark and reward longer and longer intervals.

Then, work on the dog touching and holding a specific spot while you manipulate it. You need to be able to pet the dog, check its hindquarters, lift its back leg, and lift its front leg while it holds the same position.

At the vet, mark and reward as well. The goal is for your dog to focus on "touch" so that it's still and comfortable while the injection or other procedure—which usually happens quickly—takes place.

## Training Tips

- As usual, take things slowly. Mark and reward as you gradually build duration.
- For more tips, refer back to the training tips for the "touch" command in Chapter 14.

# Ear Cleaning

## Prerequisites
None

## Practical Application
Ear infections are common in most dogs, especially those that like the water.

## Lure/Prompt
A lot of ear-cleaning training is super-easy. Make sure your dog sits or lies down in a comfortable spot. Then get it comfortable with you

petting its head, before you move on to massage and play with its ears. When that's going well, start lifting the ears up.

Put an ear-cleansing or saline solution on a rag. Continue to pet and lift up your dog's ear, using the rag to first massage and then clean the outer ear. As the dog becomes comfortable with that, start moving further into the ear canal and cleaning that.

## Training Tips

• As always, take it slow, establishing and re-establishing trust.

# Urinating on Cue

## Prerequisites

"Go potty" and "hurry up" are the most common cues.

## Practical Application

It's time for Potty Training 201. Sometimes you're in a hurry and the dog's not.

You and your dog may be traveling. Sometimes you may want your dog to go to the bathroom as soon as possible.

It's also a good plan to get your dog in the habit of taking the opportunity to use the bathroom whenever one arises. This can be especially useful if you live in an apartment and don't have a backyard.

## Lure/Prompt

Give your dog the "hurry up" command just before it starts to go to the bathroom.

Walk outside and watch. Your dog will start spinning in circles, sniffing around, and putting its rear end down near the ground. Just before it starts going, say "Hurry up." When the dog finishes, mark and reward.

## Training Tips

- Don't interrupt your dog during the task, even or especially with a reward.
- If you start getting overly excited, your dog may lose concentration and won't empty its bladder. This will lead to an accident later.

# THE TAIL END

As mentioned earlier in the book, the Greek lyric poet Archilochus famously noted that "We don't rise to the level of our expectations. We fall to the level of our training." If this is true for humans, it's even truer for puppies.

The habits your puppy forms will stick with it into adulthood. Take the reins and teach it how to behave. Train your dog effectively and you'll reap the benefits for years to come.

Puppies aren't Furbies. There's no such thing as "set it and forget it" in dog training. You need to continually maintain what you've already worked on. And always link learning and conditioning to clear-cut goals or overcoming specific weaknesses.

Ultimately, however, this process is what makes building a relationship with your dog so rewarding. You have the life of another being in your hands and the power to make it better—enriching your own life at the same time.

## FINAL TIPS

- Training is about quality over quantity.
- Success follows your efforts.
- Discomfort—some discomfort, that is—is the price of success.
- If you're in a hole, stop digging!

Better training makes for happier dogs and happier owners. That means fewer people abandoning dogs because they're "difficult," fewer dogs lonely or euthanized in shelters, more kids with a wonderful companion, and better relationships between everyone in the family and our canine friends. It's a win-win-woof (that means "win" in dog)-win.

Don't be misled into thinking training is easy. But it's worth it. You need to structure your training for success. In sports, the cycling and recycling of aspects of training, from basic to advanced, is called periodization. Like athletes, you and your dog have to keep practicing between games—or visits to the local brewpub—if you're going to remain proficient.

When training, always prepare. Don't go out and work your dog haphazardly. Utilize the appropriate tools whenever you need them.

If you're working a training program and aren't seeing results, you need to reevaluate. Going down a path where there's been little improvement won't yield more improvement. Find out what the issue is and move toward a solution.

In training, you're always working with both your dog and yourself. Each of you will feel frustrated at times. You'll be frustrated when you don't understand how to communicate what you want to your dog. Your dog will be frustrated because it doesn't clearly understand what you're trying to explain to it.

That's going to happen, and that's okay. What's important is to continue moving forward. Dog training is a journey, not a destination.

Training your dog is a little like being an entrepreneur starting a business. One day life is great. The next day, everything is crashing and burning before you.

## For More Help

Many people develop a cupboard full of dog training tools but don't know how and when to use them. Sometimes, your otherwise-

# Life With A Dog

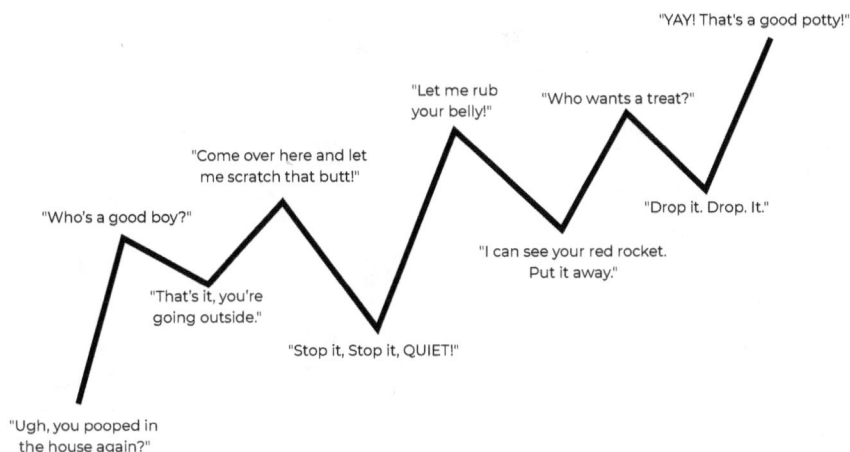

"YAY! That's a good potty!"

"Let me rub your belly!"

"Who wants a treat?"

"Come over here and let me scratch that butt!"

"Who's a good boy?"

"Drop it. Drop. It."

"I can see your red rocket. Put it away."

"That's it, you're going outside."

"Stop it, Stop it, QUIET!"

"Ugh, you pooped in the house again?"

trained dog will still act in ways that perplex or frustrate you, and you need to know what to do. Instead of scratching your head, turn to MindYourPaws.com for resources to further support turning your puppy into the perfect pet.

A structured, balanced training program is the best way to give you and your dog a great life together. Get to it, and while you're at it, don't forget to have fun!

mindyourpaws.com

# ABOUT THE AUTHOR

If there's anyone who can teach an old dog new tricks, it's Jason R. Toy. Jason got his PhDog after apprenticing with a highly respected dog trainer, then went on to found Canine Scholars to share his practical, lighthearted brand of dog training with the world.

Now he has written *Mind Your Paws*, a complete guide to navigating the confusing decisions facing perplexed puppy parents. Based in the Carolinas, Jason is also creator of the Puppy Potty Log app and the Mind Your Paws video course to accompany this book. His pet pooches enjoy watching the videos almost as much as playing fetch.